THE WINNING EDGE 4

Traders' & Investors' Greater Success

By Adrienne Laris Toghraie, MNLP, MCH

TRADERS PRESS®
INCORPORATED
PO BOX 6206
GREENVILLE, SC 29606

Books and Gifts for
Traders and Investors.

ISBN 0-934380-82-1

Published March 2002
By Traders Press, Inc.®

Editing and Cover Design by
Rick Morgan

Traders Press, Inc.®
PO Box 6206
Greenville, SC 29606

Serving Traders since 1975

Publisher's Comments

It is generally recognized that there are three main areas with which the trader needs to be concerned in order to become successful in the pursuit of trading excellence: the method or system used, risk control or money management, and the emotional and mental aspect. Not uncommon is the mistake of putting more emphasis on the first of these three aspects, to the exclusion or the lack of emphasis on one or both of the others. Many traders feel that if they can just find a method or a system that consistently generates profitable signals, they will automatically be successful, and they forget the other areas, especially the mental and emotional preparation.

Many experienced traders with whom I have discussed this idea feel that the emotional side of trading is by far the most important, albeit the most neglected. They understand that this aspect of trading must be mastered and dealt with effectively before the others.

Adrienne Toghraie is exceptionally well qualified to offer much needed help in this area to new and veteran traders alike. Her qualifications as a trader's coach go back for many years. She has been instrumental in the success of many a trader who came to her for help.

I am proud that *Traders Press* was selected to publish and distribute this edition of Adrienne's "Winning Edge" series. I am confident that it will make a worthwhile and significant contribution to your own success as a trader.

Edward D Dobson

Edward D. Dobson, President
Traders Press, Inc.

March 8, 2002

Greenville, SC

iii

TRADERS PRESS, INC.®
PO BOX 6206
GREENVILLE, SC 29606

Publishers of:

A Complete Guide to Trading Profits (Paris)
A Professional Look at S&P Day Trading (Trivette)
A Treasury of Wall Street Wisdom (Editors: Schultz & Coslow)
Ask Mr. EasyLanguage (Tennis)
Beginner's Guide to Computer Assisted Trading (Alexander)
Channels and Cycles: A Tribute to J.M. Hurst (Millard)
Chart Reading for Professional Traders (Jenkins)
Commodity Spreads: Analysis, Selection and Trading Techniques (Smith)
Comparison of Twelve Technical Trading Systems (Lukac, Brorsen, & Irwin)
Complete Stock Market Trading and Forecasting Course (Jenkins)
Cyclic Analysis (J.M. Hurst)
Dynamic Trading (Miner)
Exceptional Trading: The Mind Game (Roosevelt)
Fibonacci Ratios with Pattern Recognition (Pesavento)
Futures Spread Trading: The Complete Guide (Smith)
Geometry of Markets (Gilmore)
Geometry of Stock Market Profits (Jenkins)
Harmonic Vibrations (Pesavento)
How to Trade in Stocks (Livermore & Smitten)
Hurst Cycles Course (J.M. Hurst)
Investing by the Stars (Weingarten)
Magic of Moving Averages (Lowry)
Market Rap: The Odyssey of a Still-Struggling Commodity Trader (Collins)
Pit Trading: Do You Have the Right Stuff? (Hoffman)
Planetary Harmonics of Speculative Markets (Pesavento)
Point & Figure Charting (Aby)
Point & Figure Charting: Commodity and Stock Trading Techniques (Zieg)
Profitable Grain Trading (Ainsworth)
Profitable Patterns for Stock Trading (Pesavento)
Short-Term Trading with Price Patterns (Harris)
Single Stock Futures: The Complete Guide (Greenberg)
Stock Patterns for Day Trading (2 volumes) (Rudd)
Stock Trading Based on Price Patterns (Harris)
Study Helps in Point & Figure Techniques (Wheelan)
Technically Speaking (Wilkinson)
Technical Trading Systems for Commodities and Stocks (Patel)
The Amazing Life of Jesse Livermore: World's Greatest Stock Trader (Smitten)
The Opening Price Principle: The Best Kept Secret on Wall Street (Pesavento)
The Professional Commodity Trader (Kroll)
The Taylor Trading Technique (Taylor)
*The Trading Rule That Can Make You Rich** (Dobson)
Trading Secrets of the Inner Circle (Goodwin)
Trading S&P Futures and Options (Lloyd)
Twelve Habitudes of Highly Successful Traders (Roosevelt)
Understanding Bollinger Bands (Dobson)
Understanding Fibonacci Numbers (Dobson)
Viewpoints of a Commodity Trader (Longstreet)
Wall Street Ventures & Adventures Through Forty Years (Wyckoff)
Winning Edge 4 (Toghraie)
Winning Market Systems (Appel)

Please contact Traders Press to receive our current catalog describing these and many other books and gifts
of interest to investors and traders.
800-927-8222 ~ 864-298-0222 ~ fax 864-298-0221 ~ TradersPress.com ~ Tradersprs@aol.com

About the Author

ADRIENNE LARIS TOGHRAIE, MNLP, MCH, is a **trader's coach,** an internationally recognized authority in the field of human development and a master practitioner of Neuro-Linguistic Programming (NLP) for the financial and business communities. She is the founder and president of *Trading on Target* and *Enriching Life Seminars,* two companies dedicated to helping traders, sales people, and other high achievers to dramatically increase profits and success in all areas of life. Using her 20 years of study in the science of Modeling Excellence/(NLP) and numerous other forms of psychological development, Ms. Toghraie has helped her clients to push through their self-imposed limitations to extraordinary and documented new levels of success.

Adrienne's articles and interviews have been featured in most of the major financial trade magazines and newspapers throughout the world. She has authored *Get A life*: *Treasure Diary for Creating Wealth and Happiness, The Winning Edge 2: Traders' and Investors' Psychological Coach in a Book, The Winning Edge 3: Traders' and Investors' Coaching to Excellence, Dear Coach: Potty Training for Traders, Brokers & Investors,* and co-authored *Traders' Secrets* with Murray Ruggiero and *The Winning Edge, How to Use Your Personal Psychological Power in Trading and Investing* with Jake Bernstein.

Adrienne's public seminars and private counseling, as well as her television appearances and keynote addresses at major industry conferences, have achieved a wide level of recognition and popularity.

Table of Contents

Section One: *Trading & Modeling Strategies*

Section Two: *Personal & Emotional Issues*

Section Three: *Sabotage Traps to Avoid*

Section Four: *Strategies for Improving your Trading*

Section Five: The Physical Side of Trading

Section Six: *Handling the Worst Things*

Section Seven: *Choosing Success*

Dedicated To

Those Who Seek, Defend and Protect:

Peace
Equality
Justice
Freedom

And to those who conquer their fears so that we can continue to enjoy a healthy economy and an abundant life.

Acknowledgments To

Rick Morgan

Who gives the TOT Bull his flair and humor.

Wendy Clouse

Who coordinated the assembly and editing
of this book and is my invaluable right hand.

Antonia Weeks

Who taught me how to write and assisted me every
Step of the way by continuously asking,
"So what are you really trying to say?"

Roger Reimer

Who was our invaluable editor.

&

**A special thanks to all of the traders who
contributed their stories, so that everyone
could learn from their lessons.**

Preface

Neuro-Linguistic-Programming is known as the science of modeling. Modeling the behavior, strategies and thinking of someone who has achieved excellence in any given field is the fastest and most effective way to achieve the same excellence yourself.

As a coach, I use models of success that I have developed over the years in working with top achievers and transfer that training to those who want to be highly successful traders themselves. Models are best understood through a series of metaphors. People relate to and understand a story better then instructions.

The following three metaphors form the basis of one of the models I use to coach traders and other high achievers to each next level of success, and is the model I used through the *Winning Edge* series of books:

1. If a farmer has a problem with his crop, the problem is usually as a result of something happening to the root of the plant.

2. In the movie "The Hoosiers," Gene Hackman plays the role of a famous college basketball coach who is reduced to working at an obscure high school after his personal issues overtook his profession. Despite his personal difficulties, he was still a great coach. He proved it by coaching a last place high school basketball team to first place in their state in a single season. He accomplished this minor miracle by concentrating on the basics.

3. When you watch coaches at the Olympics train athletes who have made a mistake, the coaches will require the athletes to repeat the same feat over and over until they have fixed the right action in their minds and muscles.

The Model

When a trader comes for coaching, he often comes with a problem that needs to be addressed. Using the model based on my three metaphors, the first step is to look for the root of the problem. That root usually has to do with some issue in the past that needs transforming or healing. Then, we take the steps necessary to conquer those issues. In the *Winning Edge* books, I explain some of the processes I use so you can do them yourself.

The continuous next steps in this model are to make certain that the client understands and can execute the basics of each new level of competence.

Then, I make them repeat their successes over and over until the experience becomes unconscious, like blinking their eyes.

As I work with individual clients and with people who attend my seminars, I observe issues that need to be addressed. Afterwards, I write about these issues and propose strategies for overcoming these problems. Many times, these issues are the same ones that I have written about in previous chapters, issues that are so basic to successful trading that they keep appearing in different forms, such as not being able to follow trading rules. I believe in approaching the basics from many different angles. Each client provides new insights in accomplishing this goal by providing me with their unique set of circumstances. You will know that you understand the basics when you are able to follow your rules consistently. In order for this to happen, you must understand the basics on an unconscious level as well as on a conscious level. In other words, your behaviors must become automatic. Once you are achieving top performance on a consistent basis, it is important that you use the *Winning Edge* series of books as a resource to reinforce good behavior.

Foreword

By Art Collins

Author of: *Top Traders Under Fire*

Put me in the Investor/Business section of a bookstore, and I am in heaven. I do not mind wading through all the shoddiness. Despite its share of myths, half-truths and outright falsehoods, there are some real diamonds within the business book "rough." I look for two categories—the how-to mechanical approach manuals, and the biographical /psychological trader profiles. Regarding the former, I would never merely follow the suggestions verbatim. I do not trust what I have not researched, for one thing. I do use such texts for inspiration, however. Some imaginative, new approach to breakouts or oscillators could send me into a research frenzy for weeks.

It is probably the latter category, however, that has provided me with the most pay dirt. Trading is such a uniquely complex and difficult experience that understanding its ramifications while in the heat of battle can be near impossible. That is why the occasional sage offering universal insight is such a rare and valuable asset.

Adrienne Laris Toghraie is such a person. She is one of the most highly recognized trader coaches and experts in the field of Neuro-Linguistic Programming. She has lectured internationally and appeared on several financial programs including CNBC.

And of course, she has written extensively, including four volumes of her *Winning Edge* series. I had somehow managed to overlook her work until someone suggested that she be a subject of my own book. From the minute we began the phone interview, I knew I was getting one of my more vital contributions.

Adrienne provided one shock of recognition after another. She outlined the typical experience of the trader in crisis. Losses are merely the most conspicuous part of the problem. Underlying them is a wide array of dysfunctional physical and psychological components, which Adrienne refers to as "The Cesspool." It is what sucks you down and keeps you off base. It also, unfortunately, feeds on itself.

Adrienne's job as a coach is to help traders regain overall balance in their lives. Each of their facets can then harmoniously support all the others. Everything is considered, including stress management and nutrition.

Adrienne shows uncanny empathy concerning such trader fundamentals as discipline and risk control. A person who loses $100,000 after having just run up a quarter of a million might be dismissed as reckless within some psychology sectors. Adrienne considers the total picture. A high degree of risk taking is a component integral to top echelon returns.

She even approaches the compulsive gambling problem in a more contextual way than traditional therapists who can only advocate total abstinence. Re-channel the compulsiveness, Adrienne suggests. Make it so the trader becomes equally obsessive about risk control, and about paying attention to habits that would support good trading.

Positive conditioning involves a series of daily choices. Get the clutter out of your office and your life, and you will be better equipped to filter out extraneous market "noise." Be cognizant of the bad habits and legacies of your upbringing. Recognize danger times when stress is particularly omnipresent. Clean up your lifestyle. In some hands, this could appear simplistic or trendy. As Adrienne recounts it, though, you can feel the connection—the personal application.

"If I were to say to you, my whole seminar is 'create your own reality,' that is the bottom line," she said in my interview. "But in order to get the experience out of it so that it is meaningful enough to apply towards higher levels of success, you need to go through a certain process."

The process is a procedure in which trader and coach, reader and author navigate together. I do not know how much of Adrienne's skill is from personal market experience, how much is from years in the psychology trenches, and how much is an innate talent. She is rather enigmatic. You get a wide array of observations about her, including the fact that she is a cat lover and a flashy dresser.

What virtually everyone agrees about her, though, is how open and nice she is. I will add my own affirmation. She devoted time and energy clueing me in on the various avenues of book promotion; something she obviously did not have to do.

I am grateful for such help, as well as for her fine contribution to my book. I am also glad just to know that she is out there--that I have a new wealth of material available to me in my bookstore.

But more than anything, I am honored that she asked me to write this forward. Thanks Adrienne, and may your faith prove justified.

SECTION 1
Trading and Modeling Strategies

Chapter 1

RECRUITING YOURSELF INTO TRADING

The Devil Made Me Do It

Recently, I was sent an e-mail about a woman who was in the Human Resources field. As the story went, the woman in the story had died and was negotiating her final destination with Saint Peter at the Pearly Gates. Saint Peter said, "Normally, we are clear on relocation, but in your case, we are going to give you an opportunity to choose. You will have the experience of both worlds so you can make your decision."

Her first stop was a day in Hell where she found herself enjoying a country club setting with friends and relatives who were having a "super fun time." Next, she spent a day in Heaven where she lived in peace and serenity while floating on a cloud. Afterwards, she said to Saint Peter, "I never thought I would be saying this, but Hell is more my style." With that decision, she was promptly escorted down to Hell where she was met by the Devil who awaited her with the satisfied grin of a winner. Looking beyond him, she saw a bleak, dismal place with nothing but suffering. Alarmed, she cried, "What's happening? I was here yesterday and this was a living paradise!" The Devil responded, "Yesterday, you were being recruited. Today, you get to experience the real thing."

Facing the Real World of Trading

Most people who enter the trading profession are recruited. They are seduced by a dream that they create in their own minds. However, that dream will not be the reality for them once they make the decision to commit. While trading is a profession that satisfies the dreams of many people, it is a living hell for those who are unprepared to do the things that are necessary to become a successful trader. The unprepared recruits who suddenly face a different reality than their dreams must adjust quickly or go under just as quickly.

The dream for most budding traders includes:
- The freedom to run their own business

3

- The independence to be on his or her personal schedule
- The full accountability for success or failure
- The opportunity to make an incredible income
- The challenge of a profession that is always changing

Let's take a look at the dream versus the reality:

1. **The Freedom to Run my Own Business**

   It is a fact that running your own business as a professional trader involves a great deal of personal and professional freedom. The dream of having this freedom is a powerful motivator for traders. Many of the people who come into trading have had the experience of working in a highly structured and controlled organizational environment. These individuals have chaffed under the watchful eyes of people who are less talented and more committed to their own personal agendas for advancement and power than the welfare of their employees or their employers. They have watched the clock as it ticks off the minutes of their lives under someone else's control and they have fantasized about the time when they would answer to no one but themselves.

   Most freedom dreamers have not acquired the actual experience of running their own business. As the old saying goes, "With Freedom comes Responsibility." With the ultimate freedom of running your own business comes the ultimate responsibility of keeping it afloat. Many people are not prepared for the level of responsibility that comes with the business of trading. The first time these traders experience a major drawdown, they are confronted with some very frightening possibilities:

   - They could suddenly be out of business
   - They may not have enough capital left to pay their immediate bills
   - They do not have a paycheck coming in next week to cover the shortfall

   Unless a trader was raised in a home where one or both parents were entrepreneurs, he will be unprepared for the realities inherent in running a trading business. The traders that I have worked with who were raised by entrepreneurs have been steeped in the risks and rewards of running their own business. They are not seduced by glowing visions of personal freedom because they understand that the freedom comes at a cost. They do not panic when business suddenly falls off because they knew it would happen sometime. Markets work not just in the charts and exchanges that are highly visible; they also operate at the dining room table where the traders live. Understanding this fact has prepared these traders for the inevitable ups and downs of their business.

   A trader named Adam was raised in a family where his father was an entrepreneur. From the time that he was in middle school, Adam was forming his own small businesses. In fact, he discovered very early that when he attempted to work in someone else's organization, he became discontented and unable to follow the prescribed organizational model or he was soon running the show. At one point, he

4

formed a trading partnership but soon discovered that he was doing all the work, assuming all the risk, and getting very little for it. Eventually, he formed his own trading business and has watched his business grow rapidly. Adam has experienced periods of loss where he has worried about his economic future, but he has the lifelong experience of being an entrepreneur to realize that certain months are slow ones. He knows that markets eventually turn around and that he can create a win situation for himself once more. As a result of this entrepreneurial history, Adam is well suited to the "dream" of being a trader.

2. **The Independence to be on my Personal Schedule**
The dream of being a trader comes with the anticipation of being able to set your own work schedule. Time independence means that you no longer have to be on a train at 6:35 a.m. or at your desk by 8:30 a.m. You can take a five-week vacation with your family to Europe if you want. And, you can set limits on the time that you spend on your work, meaning that you can work four hours per day or fifteen hours per day if you choose to. You own your time and that is a tremendously liberating and seductive recruiting tool for the profession of trading.

If this vision is the dream, what is the reality? It is true that you are on no one else's schedule. But, if you know very much about running a business, you know that you had better have a schedule if you are going to survive, much less succeed. Yes, it will be your schedule, but it will probably not be the one that you had in mind when you signed on. Instead of having to start work at 8:30 a.m., you might not start until 9:00 a.m., but your schedule might require that you work until 8:00 p.m. each day.

Full-time professional traders make a time commitment in the beginning stages of their trading career that is as great as any beginning professional. This commitment includes the time required to read hundreds of books and articles about trading, to attend seminars and trade shows, to work on your psychology, to develop and back-test a trading system and to paper trade. Much of this activity is done merely in the preparation to trade, which means that you are not even in business for a long period of time, perhaps even years. Once a trader is actually in business (i.e. is finally trading his system), he is definitely on the clock. If he trades longer-term positions, he may not want to take vacations and his spouse may be begging for a long weekend away rather than enjoying the five week vacation in Europe. That dispels the idea of the free time in the dream.

3. **Full Accountability for Success or Failure**
For the individual who wants to have full credit for his own successes and failures, trading is definitely going to fulfill the recruiting promises. The problem is that most non-entrepreneurial traders have never experienced the failure part of the reality in their dreams much less in their previous reality. A serious loss in the market can send a veteran trader into a tailspin. It can do much worse to a neophyte trader. If he wants to take full responsibility for that major loss, he may not be prepared for the self-doubt, fear, and guilt that can come cascading down on him as a result.

The reality is that few new traders are prepared for major success or major failure unless they have done a great deal of work on their psychology. It also helps to be an individual with one of those rare dispositions that takes everything in stride or to have an entrepreneurial background.

Brad came from a highly privileged background where everything came easily to him. As a result, Brad was lulled into the self-delusion that his successes were the result of his superior intelligence and character. He was happy to take full credit for them, however modestly he posed for his rewards. Since he had never failed at anything, he believed that hypothetical failures would be small, painless, and self-directed instructions to improvement in his techniques. Was he ever in for a shock? Trading was such a painful experience for him that he lasted about three months before he rediscovered an old passion and followed it.

4. **The Opportunity to Make an Incredible Income**
The field of professional trading has a goodly number of rags to riches stories, enough, in fact, to provide endless copy for the devil himself. If you go to your local bookstore, you can pull numerous books from the shelves that are written by or about self-proclaimed wizards. When asked why he robbed banks, a notorious gangster once replied, "That's where the money is!" Since there is easily as much money in the markets, it follows that someone will be making it. So, "Why not you?" is how the recruiting poster lures new traders into the game.

The reality is that it takes a tremendous commitment to be an average good trader who makes a living at trading. The incredible incomes go to that handful of traders who have taken the extraordinary steps to reach mastery or who were positioned for great success through a combination of great luck and the mental stability that is perfectly suited to trading.

It is more likely that a trader who has not made a great commitment to learning the business and/or who is not blessed with an entrepreneurial history will struggle to make a living at trading rather than reap windfall profits each year.

5. **The Challenge of a Profession that is Always Changing**
No doubt about it, trading is always changing. That may look like a benefit on the way in, but it is often the undoing of a trader who is on the way out. Just when you thought that all of your research and paper trading has perfected your approach, you discover that things are about to change. That is what happened to Ross. He had a system that made a small fortune for him in the booming markets of the past. As the economy slowed, suddenly Ross discovered that he could no longer make money with his system. His situation is not as dire as the floor traders who have worked in the pits for years making tremendous incomes. As exchanges are converting to electronic trading formats, open outcry markets are coming under increasing attack. It is one thing to have to change your system, but it is entirely another thing to have to change your entire way of trading.

To be resilient enough to weather continual change is a gift. Nevertheless, even the most gifted can need a break from change or wear out due to an excess of change.

Conclusion

If you recruited yourself into trading by subscribing to the beliefs outlined in this article, you may have already begun to see how you have been duped. The army recruiter in the movie, "Private Benjamin," showed the naive young widow, Goldie Hawn, pictures of condominiums at an oceanfront resort. "This is the New Army," he told her ingenuously. Like Private Benjamin, you may have seen the top one-half of one percent of the trading world and extrapolated it into the "new world of trading." The real world of trading is as demanding and unforgiving as it ever was. To be successful over time, you still have to put in long hours on a rigorous schedule, you still have the opportunity to fail completely and be totally responsible for losing everything while trying to dodge the changes that come like a tsunami. There is no dream – only the reality that commitment, hard work, flexibility, and self-discipline will eventually allow you to make a decent living in trading.

Chapter 2

A TRADER "IN-TRAINING"

Top trading is all about performance. To trade well over an extended period of time requires consistently good performance. Often, a first time performer or trader can produce spectacular results from an initial burst of energy, beginner's luck, or a fearlessness that comes from inexperience. But duplicating those results day after day requires enormous stamina and experience plus the right psychology to deal with fear, pain, failure, and success. This point is where training comes in.

To perform well, you have to be healthy. Top performance requires an abundant and reliable supply of energy. Abundant energy provides you with the strength to make the correct decisions and deal with the results of those decisions. The only way for a trader to create that supply of energy is to go into training, much like an Olympic athlete or someone who is required to provide consistent performance. In interviews with top performing traders, I have been impressed with the level of personal training these traders commit themselves to. They take their physical and psychological health very seriously, as if it were a major part of their trading capital. Without the performance quality of their trading, their monetary trading capital could disappear overnight.

The Trading Givens

There are certain things that should be understood as far as a trader is concerned. A trader must have a tested system or methodology including money management rules. Beyond that, there is the need for the right psychology, which needs to be balanced physically, mentally, and emotionally. In order for this balance to occur, a trader must be healthy. To achieve good health depends upon choices that are made every day. All day, every day, a trader is faced with an unending series of choices that determine his physical and mental health:

- Waking up and starting the day in a frenzy or starting the day with a plan
- Starting the day with exercise or rushing to the screen

- What to eat for breakfast - the protein drink or the donut and coffee
- What to have for lunch - the tuna on whole wheat or the greasy hamburger and fries
- Taking time out midday to relax and recharge or pushing on until exhaustion comes
- Passing up drugs and/or alcohol or giving in to temptation
- Spending time with your family or watching television
- Getting at least 7 hours of sleep or working on charts until midnight

More than anything else, the choices you make all day determine whether you are in training or not. Each individual choice may look inconsequential at the time, but a single bad choice can derail your training for hours, days, or even longer. Poor individual choices that derail your training can sabotage your trading results immediately or over time. The accumulation of bad choices, however, can permanently sabotage your results. This occurs by creating imbalances in your life that can suddenly and forcefully pull you in unexpected directions. Here are some individual examples of people who were not able to perform at their top level because their lives became unbalanced:

1. Ed Muskie was a United States Senator from Maine who was performing very well in a race for the Democratic nomination for the Presidency. In the final days of the New Hampshire primary, after becoming depleted by the physical and emotional stresses of the campaign, he emotionally fell apart before a crowd of reporters. This scene was portrayed as a sign of great weakness and his campaign folded up like a deck chair.

2. Elvis Presley was arguably the most famous rock and roll star in the world. He was undone by his penchant for donuts and drugs. His out-of-control eating habits and his reliance on prescription stimulants and sedatives were largely the result of untreated emotional issues. Emotional issues when left untreated will almost always lead to unhealthy physical choices.

3. One of my trader clients had failed to pay attention to his wife for many years as he had developed his successful trading business. He came to me for help when he returned home one day to find that his wife had moved out. After years of successful trading, he began losing on every trade and was in danger of losing everything that he had accumulated.

We are going to look at how the choices you make can affect your health. We are also going to look at steps that can be taken to prevent sabotaging your results. I want you to think of a pit that we are going to call "The Cesspool." In this cesspool, you will find all of your fears, anxieties, frustrations, weaknesses, stresses, and poor health.

Once in the pit, it is difficult to get out of and as more time passes and you sink deeper into "The Cesspool," it becomes increasingly difficult to get out of. Sometimes, even if you are doing the right things, a combination of physical stressors can put you in the pit. As an example, I worked with a trader who averaged $500,000 per year until he changed his trading pit. Parts of his life were quite good, but he got too little exercise and did not always make the best choices in selecting foods. At home, his three small children created a stressful environment that was not conducive to supporting this major change in his trading. The result of this combination of stressors was a significant down turn in his trading.

Health is not a Democracy

In a Democracy, we are born with equal political rights. However, we are not born with equal levels of natural health. Everyone functions on his or her unique health scale. For example, one person is sickly and cannot perform to a high level physically, while another individual is extremely healthy and can increase his physical abilities with very little effort. It is important to note that when we talk about increasing performance, we are talking about increasing performance relative to your personal scale and not to some standard performance scale.

The same reasoning applies to health. Some individuals can abuse themselves and get away with it. They were either born with a better immune system than their contemporaries or they improved their immune system while developing into an adult. You must take care to compare yourself only with yourself and not with other people when it comes to health issues. If you start making better choices for yourself, you will be in a training regimen that belongs to you. As you continue to follow this regimen, you will see the improvements relative to your individual performance. It is also important to note that excuses are not going to change the situation. You can justify and excuse yourself right out of health, but the fact remains that if you become ill, you have no choice about taking time out to care for yourself.

This self-assessment is my measure of how deeply you are into your training or how deeply you are in "The Cesspool." By taking this assessment and scoring it, you can see where you are now and you can compare your current results with your results as you improve your training. This is a very instructive exercise to give to someone who knows you very well to see how he or she would answer the questions about you. You might not be able to recognize the person they are describing as yourself.

Your "In–Trader Training" Evaluation

Negative Energy Issues

First, highlight the "Negative Energy Issues."
And give each a value of minus 1-5 with 5 being the worst.

1. **Health issues**
   - Addictive behaviors – alcohol - gambling - hard drugs - smoking - sex
   - Chronic conditions – pain - stress - sleep deprivation - inactivity
   - Low adrenal/immune function
   - Prescription drugs
   - Serious accident – illness

2. Dietary issues
- Dieting in excess - refined sugars - flours - rice - pasta - fatty foods with
- preservatives
- Stimulants – caffeine
- Eating disorders – overeating - unbalanced diet

3. Relationship issues
- Criticism of – self or others
- Distrustful of – self or others
- Family problems – parents - marital - children - significant other - extended family
- Lack of solid friendships
- Abuse – physical - mental - sexual

4. Emotional issues
- Past issues – abandonment – did not feel loved and or accepted – lives in the
- negative past
- Depression
- Diagnosed disorders - undiagnosed disorders
- Disorientation /delusions
- Negative feelings – fear - anger/rage - anxiety - guilt - jealousy - greed -
- unworthiness - unloved - lonely
- Represses negative emotions
- Unable to feel/express love
- Unresolved conflicts – trauma - violence
- Perfectionism

5. Environmental Issues
- Disorganization / Messiness
- Disruption / Interruption
- Negative co-worker environment
- Annoying noise
- Poor air quality
- Working with computers

6. Home Problems
- Children / Teenage problems
- Death of loved one
- Separation / Divorce
- Financial problems
- Having a baby
- Illness in family
- Lack of emotional support
- Moving

7. **Trading Issues**
   - Trading without a plan
   - Inadequate trading resources
   - Lack of trading discipline - breaking rules - over/under trading
   - Money management problems
   - Time distribution issues - over-working - unbalanced life

8. **Character issues**
   - Does not keep agreements - betrayal - cheating - lying - stealing
   - Inflexibility / Procrastination / Impatience
   - Lack of kindness
   - Laziness

Positive Energy Issues

Next, highlight the "Positive Energy Issues."
And give each a value of plus 1-10 with 10 being the best.

1. **Healthy choices**
   - Healthy – diet and supplements
   - Regular – meditations – exercise – rest – relaxation – vacations

2. **Emotional Health**
   - High self values – self confidence – self esteem – self worth
   - Fulfilling activities – social – play – hobbies – community
   - Handling past issues

3. **Mental Stimulation**
   - Puzzles - math problems - games
   - Learns new things unrelated to trading—non-trading books
   - Learns new things related to trading—trading books - journals - courses - seminars
   - Travel

4. **Spiritual life**
   - Member of spiritual community
   - Daily Prayers /Affirmations
   - Sense of being whole and connected

5. **Relationships**
   - Loves – self - people
   - Loving – family – partnership – friends – pets

Add up your score of minuses and pluses to see if you are in "The Cesspool" or "In-Trader Training." Improve your score each week until you see a noticeable difference in your trader performance.

Conclusion

You have taken the "In-Trader Training" Evaluation and have scored it based upon your performance. Have you managed, by virtue of your daily choices, to stay in training? Or are you deep in "The Cesspool?" Not only do you know where you stand right now, you also know what you need to do to get yourself into training for your own standard of peak performance. Like professional athletes or performers, you will train every day to put yourself in a state of high energy with the physical and emotional resourcefulness that you can call upon when you need to make good decisions and handle the demands of a successful, long-term trading career.

Chapter 3

MODELING TOP TRADERS

Remember when you wanted to conquer the world, when nothing could stop you from becoming a Top Trader? With a passion for success you developed your system, and over time you began to produce consistent and comfortable returns. You have a supportive family, your dream home, two cars and a country club membership. Comfortable you may be, but a Top Trader you are not.

If you have not yet lost the dream of being a Top Trader, you might wonder what it takes to be one. After all, you have worked very hard to get this far. Wouldn't it be great to take the next leap. The answer is that the difference between a Top Trader and an Average Good Trader is a very small difference indeed. I have worked closely with a fair number of genuine Top Traders, and I can tell you that to be a Top Trader, you do NOT have to be:

- extraordinarily intelligent
- highly educated
- very lucky
- from a happy and well-functioning family
- brilliant at math
- well-connected
- good-looking

Giving up the Dream

If you do not have to be an exceptional person with exceptional resources, you still do have to be willing to take calculated risks. For many traders, the accomplishment of becoming an Average Good Trader is an exceptional accomplishment. But if your goal was to be a Top Trader, and you traded in your goal for security, the part of you that needs that fulfillment will feel like it is in a state of paralysis. Eventually, you will reach that point where even your secure world will start to crumble.

Richard had dreamed of being a Top Trader. After getting off to a good start, he soon achieved a respectable level of success. Within a brief period of time he had married, fathered two children, and bought a home. Life was comfortable for him and his Top Trader goal was within reach. Then, he experienced his first major draw-down. Suddenly, Richard saw what he could lose and he was frightened. He was afraid to take any additional risks because it might mean that he would not be able to keep up with his responsibilities. As a result, Richard forged an unwritten agreement between his trading and his life. He agreed to do what was necessary to maintain his trading at the current level and life would give him what was necessary to keep up the status quo.

This arrangement would have been sufficient to make Richard content but for one fact: he knew that being a Top Trader was the main source of his passion and his reason for being a trader in the first place. He had let go of his dream and what he had in return was security. The security was good for his family and for a part of him that needed it, but not good for that part of Richard that wanted to live life fully.

Inside, Richard's disenchantment began to gnaw away at his spirit. He found it harder and harder to face his trading and his profits slipped away. His comfortable agreement unraveled. After a while, instead of being a Top Trader or even an Average Good Trader, Richard was barely making a living at trading.

So, what are some of the components that Richard was missing?

A Continual Winning Strategy

Marc is a Top Trader who has never given up his dream. From the very start, he knew that he was going to be a Top Trader. Although he did not know the exact steps to take to reach his goal, he knew from experience that each time he overcame a hurdle or conquered a personal limitation, there were lessons to be learned and that an opportunity would open up for him. So, Marc decided to find the right teachers for each step of the way. As a result of this strategy, Mark advanced one notch at a time. Although he does not possess a super intellect, and he is not a great scholar, he is very skilled at getting the best from the best. As Marc progressed in his career, he hired the best and learned from them.

Each time he found himself at a plateau, he discovered how to get off of the plateau. Using this strategy, he realized that he had reached a limit in his trading results by relying on his methodology. The only new territory left to explore was to learn to have a better relationship with himself. Marc realized that he needed to overcome the issues of his past that were holding him back, such as his limiting beliefs, his internal conflicts and his fears. At this point, he became conscious of the importance of psychology to his trading performance. With coaching, he transformed his limiting psychological issues into a psychological base that would support exceptional trading. At present, he is not only exceptionally good at bringing in trading capital, and creating money for his clients, but after years of siphoning off the knowledge from his mentors, he is now a mentor for others. He says that now being a teacher gives him what he needs to continually grow to the next level of success. And, he is earning around ten million dollars a year.

Unlimited Beliefs

Sam is a young Top Trader who once viewed himself as short, unattractive, and totally lacking in personal appeal and charisma. Nevertheless, he decided that he wanted to be a top money manager. He commenced his career on high hopes and extremely low funds. He decided that if he were going to attract investors, he would need to bring in the largest returns since he felt he wasn't sales savvy. He did not know that the average good money manager brings in 20%, so without that limiting belief he started to bring in more than 100% on family money. Even though he had limiting ideas about himself, he did not have limiting beliefs that he was not going to be a Top Trader. So, with virtually nothing in hand as far as his own capital for trading, Sam took every cent he had and hired me as his trading coach.

Like Eliza Doolittle with Professor Higgins to transform him, Sam learned to transform his opinion about his appearance. First we changed his feelings about the way he viewed his height, since that seemed to be a major issue. Instead of seeing his height as a limitation, he learned that many great men in the past stood no taller than he did and that many great men today are shorter than he is. He also learned that while he was not physically the man that would make women swoon, he could be charismatic about using his energy to attract people. The right energy could attract not only women and men to him, but investors, as well. He learned that he must take the initiative to meet people in a way that would make them want to seek him out. Each and every lesson was a difficult one for Sam, but because of his determination and his laser-like focus, he has become a top money manager. He needed to feel that he was as tall and attractive as the money he earned in order for people to believe in him enough to trust him with their money.

Finding Teachers who can Teach

Elliott was a Top Trader on the floor who came in from the cold and is now trading off the floor. He started as a floor trader by knocking on doors and by schmoozing people at trader hangouts. By making friendships and using his charm, he extracted information from these traders and learned all he possibly could about floor trading. The more information he obtained in this fashion, the more he increased his abilities and position until he was working as an independent floor trader. Long before he would need to leave the floor, he decided to take the next step and become an off the floor trader.

Applying the same strategy to this move that he did to getting on the floor, he used his charisma to seduce others to teach him about trading off the floor. But, he discovered that the information he derived from charming people was not enough to get him started. So, Elliott started hiring people to teach him. When we worked together and he had recapped who he had hired to teach him, I realized much of what he learned was not going to make him successful off the floor. Great traders are not necessarily great teachers. Great marketers and seminar leaders don't always give information that will make you a highly successful trader. Once he was directed to the right teachers he was on his way to achieving success as an off the floor trader. Now, Elliott owns two separate mansions and through his organization, he supports twenty people in an affluent life-style. From his trading on his own account, he makes in excess of two and a half million dollars each year.

Modeling these Top Traders

From these three Top Traders, you can extract some of the qualities that it takes to be a Top Trader:

1. Keep in the forefront of your mind your dream and your goals. Make sure you never take them for granted. Review them often.
2. Make sure your beliefs are in alignment with your dreams and goals. Strong supportive beliefs in the best of yourself and your ability to achieve your dreams and goals are the foundation for building success.
3. Hurdles are part of the journey and with each hurdle there is a valuable lesson to learn. Think of them as opportunities for growth.
4. Find traders who are successful in the trading that you want to do and model them.
5. Find teachers who know how to teach. Ask traders who are successful to give recommendations on good teachers.
6. Find a traders coach who you feel comfortable with, who will assist you in eliminating the sabotage that is holding you back, and will be there for you to keep achieving new levels of success.
7. Whenever you are on a new plateau, think of it as a stepping stone to the next level. The minute you stop growing you set up the environment for sabotage.
8. Always work on a better relationship with yourself by overcoming your fears and conflicts.
9. Charismatic energy is the best energy for having a good relationship with yourself and other people. This energy will bring out the passion in you, which will motivate you to focus on your dreams.
10. Mentoring for others is one of the best ways to learn new lessons for yourself. Teaching will open you up to a part of yourself that needs to learn and grow.

Conclusion

Top traders have a formula for being on top and when you apply this formula, you too can also reach high levels of success. To be at this elitist status requires you to bring out the best in yourself and sometimes that best is not enough. But, if you do what Top Traders do, think how they think and work as hard as they do, you are more likely to reach your dreams and goals. The important thing to realize is that by modeling on these Top Traders the road is not as rough.

_____

Chapter 4

MENTORS FOR TRADERS

One of the most common regrets that I hear from my trader clients is the lack of mentoring received in their professional lives. They regret not having the support and guidance of a trusted person to whom they can talk about their trading problems, fears, experiences, and feelings. What they miss is someone who can give them advice, correct them when they are making mistakes, protect them from danger, teach them the secrets of doing things well, watch over them, care about their progress, and take pleasure and pride in seeing their eventual success.

If you look closely at the requirements for the job of mentoring, you begin to realize that the model for a mentor is a good, supportive, loving and wise parent-figure. In fact, a mentor is a parent-like teacher for an adult who no longer needs a parent. Just because, we have become fully responsible for our lives does not mean that we no longer need support and guidance. We need this mentoring support for the rest of our lives. Why, then, do so many traders feel that they do not have mentors or access to mentors? Why do they feel so isolated and lonely, the result of having no one around who takes an active interest in their professional and personal lives?

The answer to this question comes from the early relationship that a trader had with his parents. It is usually the case that the parent who is the same sex as the trader is the most significant and influential parent-mentor model for the trader. If that parent does not take an active interest in teaching the young trader how to grow into a productive, well-balanced, happy, and responsible adult, then the trader will have no future model of a mentoring relationship. Later on, that adult trader may have a very difficult time finding a mentor because he cannot recognize an obvious potential relationship. Furthermore, even if he finds a mentor, he may be unable or unwilling to ask for support and guidance. Instead, he may resist the assistance, even if it is the very finest help that he could receive because it is a way of getting back at his own father for not mentoring him.

A Mentor Dad

Recently, I visited the home of one of my clients. This trader, Dave, has a three-year-old son whom he loves deeply. Wherever he goes, Dave takes his son. He has already taught him how to catch a ball, swim, tease the cat, and a host of minor masculine activities. In return, the three-year-old son idolizes his father. When Dave bought a new red work shirt to wear around home, the little boy pestered his mother for days until she finally located a red shirt just like his dad's shirt. That little boy walks and talks like his trader dad and wants to be just like him in every way. In short, Dave has started his son on a life-long path of having a mentoring relationship.

You can see what would have happened if Dave had ignored his son until he was old enough to be interesting and helpful. In fact, many fathers never take an active interest in their sons because they use the excuse that they are either too busy or they never had the experience of being mentored by their own fathers. The result is a young man who does not have a sense of having people to whom he can go for advice, support, and guidance.

What's so important about having a mentor as a trader?

"So, I don't have a mentor," you say. "So what? What difference does it make?" The answer is that it makes a great deal of difference. From my professional experience and observation in counseling traders over the past twelve years, I have found that traders who have mentors do better as traders for the following reasons:

- Having a mentor allows traders to seek help when it is needed, which is a vital resource and one that provides traders with a competitive edge.
- If traders are heading for trouble, a mentor can help to steer them in the right direction.
- A mentor can save a trader a great deal of time by not having to repeat the same mistakes that he made or common mistakes that most new traders make.
- A mentor not only saves a trader a great deal of money by preventing losses, he can also make a great deal of money for a trader by guiding him to the best trading decisions.
- A mentor can protect a trader's career by providing him with emotional support. Even the most technical mentoring provides emotional support because it reduces anxiety, increases confidence, and allows the trader to feel that he is not alone.
- Traders with mentors are more disciplined and good discipline is the backbone of successful trading. Good discipline comes from having a strong sense of purpose and self-worth, which are side benefits of having a mentor.
- A mentor can steer a trader to other valuable resources that might have been previously unavailable or unknown to the trader.
- A mentor can act as a safety valve for a trader who is feeling pressure and is unable or unwilling to share his feelings with his family.

This list is only a sampling of the benefits that accrue to a trader who has a mentor.

Suppose you do not have a mentor and you feel that you are not in an environment where you can find a suitable mentor?

Finding a Mentor

Have you ever been asked by a friend to retrieve something for him from a room in his home? After you have searched for the requested item unsuccessfully, your friend comes to rescue you and you find that the sought-after item was plainly within your sight the entire time. If so, you were probably looking for something without knowing what it looked like or what it really was. That is the situation for many traders who are looking for a mentor: they are not really certain what they are looking for or what a mentor really looks like.

What is a mentor? How would you recognize a mentor if you saw one? First, let's define a mentor: A mentor is a person who teaches, guides, and supports you in your efforts. You must have great confidence in the advice and guidance you receive from your mentor so that you will have no qualms about following his advice. A good mentor gives value to your life, providing you with the kind of information that makes you a better person or gives you the resources to develop a particular skill or ability. A potential mentor can be someone who is or could be:

- any age, sex, or occupation - potential mentors come in all shapes, colors, and sizes
- a pillar of his community excelling at everything he touches or he may not be very astute in any areas other than the one you are pursuing. Of course, it is probably better that he is someone whom you respect outside of his area of expertise because his influence may also extend to other areas of your life.
- a person you know very well, but never thought would be interested in helping you
- a co-worker
- a contact you have in your industry
- a friend of the family
- a relative
- a total stranger to you now, but someone whom you respect and would like to meet and get to know

Direct Mentors

All of these listed potential mentors are what I call "direct" mentors. You can meet and talk to them directly and receive one-on-one advice and support. They are genuine people who are accessible to your requests for help. There is a give-and-take relationship in your personal exchanges. Recognize the people in your life that may be sources for mentoring.

Indirect Mentors

Indirect mentors are people who instruct from a distance. You can access their wisdom, experience, and support through their written or spoken words. You may have access to them through seminars, books, or tapes.

You can develop a relationship with these indirect mentors by getting to know them so well that you can actually have conversations with them in your head. When you know enough about how a person thinks, you will hear answers to your questions as if they were directly from him.

A Mentor Versus a Role Model

Another alternative to a direct mentor is a role model. People of action and achievement, who become famous for their self-discipline and successes, become role models when they are neither directly or indirectly accessible as teachers and/or coaches. A role model is someone whose life, ability, or achievement is an inspiration to you. They may not be accessible to you directly or indirectly, but your imagination alone can come up with their strategies for success.

For example, Benjamin Franklin can be a great indirect mentor. He spent his life writing about the lessons that he had learned. Franklin was eager to mentor as many people as he could reach. On the other hand, George Washington is a great role model. His life was a study in taking the high road, doing the right thing, and accepting the challenge to greatness. Although he wrote a fair amount during his lifetime, his written legacy is not what we use to learn from him.

Trading Mentor and Role Models

Our ever-increasing technology benefits us with more possibilities for finding mentors and role models. Now, most of the major financial magazines offer expert advice for free. The ever-increasing published works of trading experts in books and magazines, as well as their expertise presented in seminars and in conferences all help to bring mentors and role models to us on a silver platter. This abundance of support and guidance is available to any seeker who is willing to feast on it. For example:

- Pristine.com
- tradingontarget.com
- moneymentor.com
- Traders.com
- futuresmag.com
- Ino.com

Conclusion

A trader who has a working relationship with a mentor has a competitive edge. The support offered by a mentor shows up in the bottom line as well as in the overall well being of a trader. Since mentors can come in many different forms, a trader has so many options from which to choose that he does not have to feel that he is "doing it all alone."

However, traders who grew up without a mentor-like relationship with their parents are often unable to recognize a potential mentor, seek his help, or utilize his support should it be offered. In order to overcome this obstacle to their success, they must be willing to work on their underlying issues and recognize the fact that mentors are available to support them.

Chapter 5

_____

MONEY AND TRADING

If you do not want to make money in trading, you will sabotage your trading results so that you lose money, or do not make as much money. The end result will be you will find yourself out of the trading business, probably sooner than later.

This relationship between trading and money is axiomatic and is easily acknowledged by traders, but is not easily adhered to. The problem arises for traders when the simple issue of making money becomes complicated, as it often does. Over time, the goal and desire to make money can easily become subordinated to any number of important issues in a trader's life. When the goal of making money loses its vitality and influence, trading results are adversely affected.

The reason that the relationship to money is complicated is because money becomes a metaphor for many, if not all, of the important issues in a trader's life. If a trader thinks about his success, he invariably measures it by the money that he makes. If he thinks about his personal power and influence, he thinks about money. Money has the power to create a trader's physical environment and to shape his relationship with his wife and children. It can determine the neighborhood in which a trader lives, the friendships that he makes, the way that he votes in the polls, and the vacations that he takes. It influences the way he eats, his health, and the level of stress in his life. I could continue with this list, but you get the point. It is not essential that money should have that much influence in a trader's life, but it is more often the case than not.

What ultimately determines a trader's relationship to money is the way that he talks about it to himself. The direction of that inner conversation ultimately determines how much money a trader makes, as well as how long and how well he stays in the game.

Your Beliefs are in the Driver's Seat

29

What drives the inner conversation about money for a trader? His beliefs do. Those beliefs and the inner conversations create the minute to minute practices and behaviors that influence everything a trader does. For example, many years ago I worked with a trader named Tom who believed that "money was the root of all evil." For him, making money translated into being evil, and Tom did not want to be evil. This limiting belief would cause him to talk himself into taking actions that limited his ability to make money.

Another trader, who experienced a string of painful losses each time he made money, believed that he could not hold on to money. As a result, he would talk himself into taking actions that caused him to lose whatever money he earned. Interestingly, neither trader had ever acknowledged these beliefs on a conscious level. It took a great deal of work to uncover these deeply held beliefs.

The first place to look for the origins of your beliefs is your family's relationship to money. Listed below are some common family beliefs. Ask yourself if they are applicable to your family and if so, how did you feel about them?

- Was money the most important thing in your family? Did all other concerns take a subordinate role to the making of money and the conservation of it? If so, how was that belief expressed?
- Was money viewed as power and used to control, manipulate, deceive, and/or extract love? If so, how was that accomplished?
- Was money viewed as a source of pain? Did family stories relate the acquisition of money to tragedies and/or personal sorrows?
- Was having money and abundance viewed as a natural and inevitable state, a source of happiness and blessing? If so, how was that view manifested?
- Was money scarce and was there never enough? Was your family poor and convinced that it deserved to be that way? If so, how was that belief put into practice?
- Was money a mystery that no one in your family seemed to understand how to make or create? Did they feel that they needed to be taken care of since they did not understand how to make money for themselves?

This listing is a small sample of the possible beliefs that families have about money. Since money becomes a metaphor for the issues of life, it can take on any meaning that you can imagine.

Money Karma

As you read through this list and ask yourself these questions, you may discover that money was a tainted commodity in your home. If that is the case, do not despair. Many of my clients who are successful traders overcame or reversed their families' relationships with money. Like a fair number of other traders who came from poor homes, one trader named Ted convinced himself that his relationship with money had nothing to do with his early experiences. Then, he managed to forge exact reverse mirror images of these old relationships in order to succeed as a trader, unaware that he was still responding to that early relationship. Like countless other traders who grew up in poverty, he had made the childhood promise to himself that he would be rich one day.

Our families' money beliefs may eventually be only one of a number of influences on our personal beliefs. A trader may develop his own relationship with money based upon his unique character and personality, which I call an individual's Money Karma. For example:

- If he is insecure, he will desperately hold onto his money, unable to spend it.
- If he is narcissistic, he will lavishly spend his and other people's money on himself. Without thoughts of giving and sharing, he will create personal losses that result in a psychological state that creates financial losses.
- If he has a hard time keeping his word, his money matters will spin out of control.
- If he is fearful about life, he will tend to lose his money easily or find it difficult to create it.
- If he is guilt-ridden, he will find ways to punish himself through money.
- If he is a liar, a thief, a philanderer, an abuser, or has some other serious character disorder, he will be dishonest with money and put himself at risk of getting caught in legal action.
- If he is manipulative, he will use money to control others. Eventually, the money will control him.
- If he craves power, he will abuse the power that money gives him and find himself alone and at risk of losing everything.
- If he needs to feel important, he will throw around his money to impress others, thus attracting people who will want to separate him from his money.

These relationships are based upon my experience as a counselor and are not offered as binding natural laws. It is quite possible for traders to start with the same character traits and create entirely different relationships with money because their self-talk is directed by varying sets of deeply held beliefs. The new belief becomes the all-powerful one because it attracts the emotions. The belief that attracts your emotions is the one to which your neurology will respond. Thus, each of us has his own unique Money Karma. It is important to recognize the status of your financial achievements and understand that the only thing holding you back from reaching the next level of achievement is a shift in your beliefs.

Money and Questions

Another way to solve your money-and-trading puzzle is to ask yourself how you believe that money solves problems for you. I find that most of my traders think that money will solve all of their problems. If a trader has a family, then money will make their life more comfortable, secure, and pleasant. The underlying assumption is that money will make their family life happy when in reality it will not cure all of the problems. If there is serious debt, then money will relieve the stress and solve that single problem. If a trader feels inadequate, unappreciated, or unsuccessful, money may help to fix those feelings.

To gain a better understanding of your relationship with money, you need to find out what problems you believe money will solve. You might also ask yourself, "Have I applied money to this problem in the past and what was the result?" Did the problem persist, reappear, take a new form, or disappear completely? If you answer these questions honestly, you may discover that money did not solve the problem at all because the problems in question were not about money. The root cause was somewhere else in your character, behavior, beliefs, or the environment where you live and work. The belief that getting a lot of money will solve all problems is merely an illusion.

Rob was convinced that if he could make a lot of money trading, his marriage would improve. He worked very hard to increase his profits, only to have his wife leave him anyway. The problems in their marriage were about intimacy, but they used money as the metaphor. While they both agreed that he was not providing her with enough money, Rob was actually withholding himself. When money failed to solve the marital problems, Rob's income quickly reverted to its previous less than stellar levels.

The Dark Side of Money

To completely understand your personal relationship with money, you will also have to look at the effects of the dark side of money. Many traders get themselves into deep trouble when they have all of the money that they thought they wanted. I have counseled many traders who have used money to abuse themselves with drugs, alcohol, food, and other addictive behaviors. They have gambled and spent money foolishly and in the process, became people they neither liked nor respected. So, while investigating your relationship with money, you must also ask yourself, "What problems does money create for me?"

The final question regarding money problems is "What problems does a lack of money solve for me?" This is an especially tough question for many struggling traders to consider because no one wants to believe that he is creating his own misery and lack of success. This question poses the issue of personal responsibility versus victimhood.

I worked with a trader named Rick who appeared to be permanently stuck in a pattern of never having enough money to cover his expenses. The stress from this pattern was very draining and Rick was constantly forced to face the prospect of having to find a new livelihood. All of this changed when Rick came to the realization that never having enough solved the problem of being too successful for his personal comfort zone. If he lived in abundance, he would have felt that he had overextended his reach, and unconsciously he feared that the result would have been a catastrophic fall from grace. Another trader feared making a great deal of money because he believed that he would have to assume too much additional responsibility and would be asked to assist family members and friends. This entire potential burden was perceived as a problem to be avoided.

Changing the Conversation

As you can see, the conversation you have with yourself about money is the engine that drives your relationship with money. This relationship in turn creates the abundance or lack of abundance in your trading. How can you change that conversation?

First, it is important to understand that nothing you are telling yourself about money is any more or less true than anything else you could be saying to yourself. For example, if you tell yourself that you are unable to hold on to your money, you are unconsciously instructing yourself to lose it. But, you could, just as easily, start telling yourself that you are a pure money magnet and money sticks to you. Then, you begin to instruct yourself to do exactly the opposite of losing money. The fact is that no reality exists beyond the one that you tell yourself is true. It is the telling of it that will make it so. The wonderful part of this process of changing your conversation is that you do not have to believe it to say it. Eventually, you will change the way you behave, which will ultimately change your belief.

Secondly, it is necessary that you take responsibility for your conversation from this point forward. Once you have honestly asked yourself the questions posed in this article, you will begin to shine a light on that conveniently concealed relationship you have with money. You will also have to conclude that circumstances are not responsible for your ability to make and manage your money. In fact, only you are. The markets will continue to do whatever they do, but you will create the catalyst for the changed belief.

Conclusion

As traders, we create our earnings potential and our ability to use those earnings in a way that will either support our lives or limit them by means of our money self-talk. This self-talk is going on constantly in our heads providing our instructions supporting our deeply held beliefs about money and what it means to us. Regardless of the results, these instructions are designed to use money to solve problems in our lives that too often have their roots elsewhere. Money then becomes a metaphor for whatever is missing. When this happens, making money becomes complicated and is no longer the goal of trading and successful trading becomes more difficult to achieve. In reality, we can be making a little money or a great deal of money in the same markets with essentially the same amount of effort, simply by taking responsibility for the way we are talking to ourselves about what money is to us.

SECTION 2
Personal and Emotional Issues

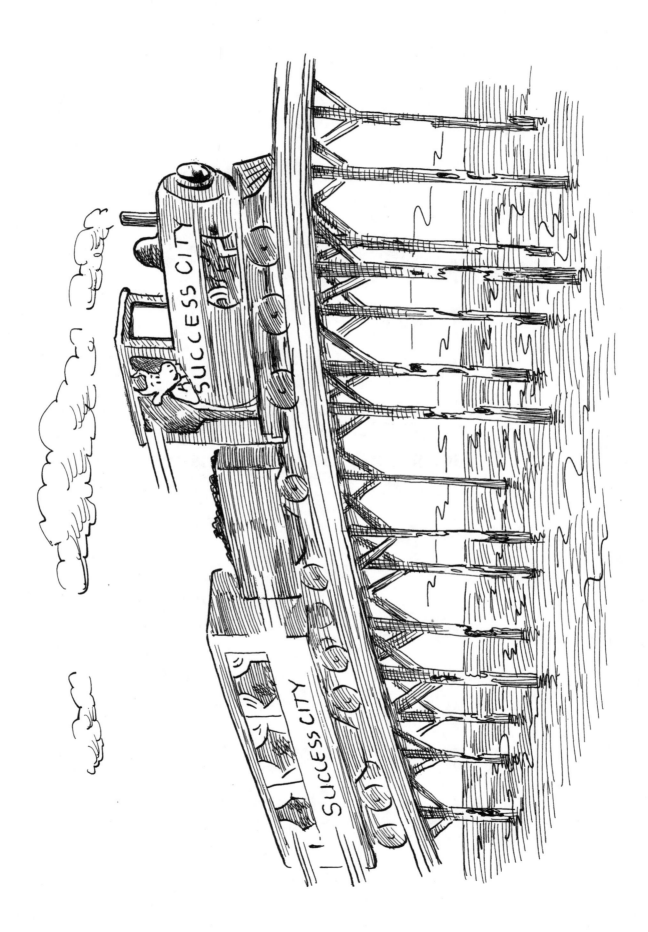

Chapter 6

HANDLING PERSONAL ISSUES

When I work with traders to help them reach their trading goals, personal issues are frequently the biggest obstacles between them and their success.

Conflicts and misunderstandings often develop between men and women as they try to create happy lives together. Issues arising between husbands and wives often cause a trader to lose focus resulting in a loss of money. Traders who are not in a significant romantic relationship can fall into the trap of preoccupying themselves with filling the emptiness they feel. Instead of focusing on their trading, these unhappy traders spend their time haunting meeting places, searching on-line, recording a video tape for a computer matching service, answering personal ads in newspapers, or staying home at night making themselves unhappy.

The end result of dealing with personal issues is stress. First, the process of finding the right relationship can be very stressful. Then, after we find a special relationship, we have the stress of working out the issues of our differences and either adjusting to those differences or accommodating behaviors that are not appealing to us. Relationship issues that are not handled in a sensible, rational and lasting way will result in negative feelings that will ultimately affect trading performance.

If you have been dealing with personal issues, these examples will illustrate that you need to take action before the personal issues become critical.

Nobody Wants Me

Tom is short and not particularly good-looking and his personality does not make him stand out in a crowd. When Tom came to me for coaching, he was a steady, good trader, but he knew that he could become a top trader if he felt better about himself. As Tom was growing up, his parents constantly told him that he had better be successful in business, because he certainly could not make it on his looks and personality. Even though Tom told himself that his parents were wrong in their assessment of his future, he could not break the mold that they had cast for him.

Tom was very clear about what he wanted - a loving wife and children. Unfortunately, Tom's social skills were insufficient to get him past an opening conversation. He felt very unappealing and alone.

Although there was nothing that we could do about Tom's height, we could work on how he felt about it. I pointed out the fact that some of the greatest lovers in history were less then average in height. Then, I gave him a long list of men in today's world that women find very attractive such as Tom Cruz, Michael Fox, and Mel Gibson. For an immediate change in appearance, I suggested a hair stylist and wardrobe consultant. For a long-term change, I suggested that Tom work out with weights at the gym.

The most important part of the impression that Tom made was not his appearance, but in how he presented himself. First, we had to reverse Tom's belief that he did not have an appealing personality. We supported self-esteem changes by having him join Toastmasters. Participating in Habitat for Humanity made him feel good about himself. I also suggested that Tom take an acting class where he could learn to act as if he were the person he wanted to be. Then, he enrolled in a comedy class where he could learn how to be amusing. I also suggested that he enroll in a modeling class where he met Alice, the woman of his dreams. The fact that she was a head taller than Tom was not a problem for her. Alice found Tom's personality to be so attractive that she found him attractive. And, yes, Tom's trading improved dramatically as a benefit.

The Honeymoon is Over

Tony and Marie could not have been happier through their courtship and honeymoon. But, after settling into their new town home, the problems began to appear quickly and began to affect Tony's trading. At night, after a long day trading, Tony wanted to be greeted by a loving wife with a clean and orderly home, and a hot home cooked meal. Instead, he arrived to a messy, disorganized house with a Hungry Man Dinner waiting for him to pull out of the freezer and cook on his own. His wife, Marie, was a fitness addict whose time at the gym took priority over her home and her husband's desire for a home cooked meal. Marie's profession took her time and energy during the day and she did not have the time and energy to be a housekeeper, too.

Tony was accustomed to his old-fashioned Italian 'momma' who knew how to create a 'homey' atmosphere. When in her neighborhood, you could smell the garlic tomato sauce simmering in her kitchen from a block away. While he missed the home that his mother created, Tony did not want Marie to be a walking advertisement for good cooking like 'Momma' was. The other benefit his mother never provided was the kind of income that Marie contributed to the household. Even though Tony recognized the financial benefits that he enjoyed from Marie's career, he was still angry with her for not creating the home of his youth. In response to his anger, Tony began to model his father's behavior and began yelling at his wife. Marie, on the other hand, came from a background where her parents discussed their issues and found Tony's yelling primitive and insulting.

When I met Tony, his trading performance was dismal and he was toying with the idea of divorcing Marie. To improve his trading, Tony needed to mend his relationship with Marie. To accomplish this, Tony had to learn to deal reasonably and rationally with his wife and reconsider his unconscious demands for his wife to take the place of his mother. Tony wanted a comfortable home, a home cooked meal, and he wanted to share these pleasures with Marie. What he had to give up were the specific means by which these goals were achieved and his need to control them.

Fortunately, Tony and Marie cooperated with the compromise solutions that I proposed. They hired a housekeeper to clean the house once a week and an organizer to establish an assigned place for everything. They agreed to cooperate and tried to keep everything in its assigned place. Marie learned to cook his mom's tomato sauce, which she made on Sunday in large quantities so she would have it available for several meals. Tony and Marie each took responsibility for cooking one meal per week. Once a week, they paid a restaurant to bring dinner to their house, one day a week they ate at a restaurant, and on Sunday they ate at Momma's house. Marie agreed to limit her gym time to early in the morning, during her lunch hour, or after dinner with Tony. She respected Tony for his shift in behavior. Instead of fighting him, she took extra care to provide Tony with the home that he wanted to have. And Tony's trading is better than ever.

Here Comes the Tribe

When everything is going well in your significant relationship, other relationship issues can take attention away from good trading performance. An infinite number of issues can develop with other family members, friends and associates. Here are some examples of other relationship issues that have been problematic for some of my clients.

Bundle of Horror

The image of a couple receiving the gift of a healthy baby is always a joyous one. But what happens if this baby has colic? The bundle of joy can turn into a bundle of horror.

Because George trades in California time, he needs to go to sleep early and get up early to have a good trading day. Gregory entered the lives of Jill and George screaming and has not stopped since. Compounding this problem, Jill is also the mother of a "terrible-two" toddler and is suffering from post-natal depression. So, George starts his trading day exhausted from lack of sleep and Jill is irritable from lack of sleep and depression. Her constant complaining disturbs his concentration while he works in his home office. After his workday, George is in a terrible mood because he has missed trading opportunities that he would normally take. At the same time, Jill desperately needs someone who will listen to her needs and relieve her from her continuous pressures.

When George called and told me about his family problems, I asked the obvious question, "Why don't you get help?" George replied that his wife did not like strangers in the house. "Besides," he said, "she has nothing to do but take care of the house and kids." George's own mother had taken care of four children in a small apartment without help. Thus, he could not understand why his wife could not handle two children in a large home with all of the modern conveniences. However, when I spoke to Jill, I discovered that George was really the one who did not want "strangers" in the house. The underlying problem was that George had an issue with spending money on help for his wife.

If George did not resolve the issues at home immediately, he was in imminent danger of losing everything and would soon find himself in the small apartment of his childhood. His mind was filled with negative anchors that were affecting his trading. But, before he could affect changes in his trading results, George needed to make major shifts in his belief systems:

1. How he viewed his wife's issues
2. Their problems with a colic baby
3. How he felt about getting help

When George looked at his beliefs, he realized that his wife's depression was equivalent to his own depression in trading and that she also needed help with a professional. While she was getting that help, they hired a loving woman from South America to care for Gregory. This woman's husband worked the night shift in a factory, so her evenings were free. Eager to learn English, she had an audiotape language course that she listened to while cradling and carrying the crying baby. The earphones that she wore helped to stifle the noise from his screaming. George and Jill also sent their two-year-old son to a day care center for four hours a day.

The money that George spent to solve his family problems was a small fraction of what he was losing by not hiring the extra help. A mere six months later, Jill is over her depression and is adding extra joy to the relationship, the baby no longer is colicky, and his two-year old is loving daycare. George is making more money then ever. It cost approximately ten thousand dollars to take care of his wife and children and seven thousand dollars to take care of his own needs. The benefit is that George now enjoys the process of making more than six times that amount in his trading.

Vampire Funeral

Dressed in black from head to toe, Randy's daughter, Sue, looked like she was going to a vampire funeral every day while she was attending high school. Her parents tried punishing, threatening, and rewarding, but nothing worked in getting her to change her style of dress. The good signs were that Sue was an excellent student and was well liked by other students. Nevertheless, Randy was afraid that his daughter's next step would be drugs, teenage pregnancy and a sexually transmitted disease. His preoccupation with her future kept him from good trading performance.

When I spoke to Sue, I found out that she chose this style of dress because she wanted to be different. I explained to her that while she might be different from the rest of the students in this school, she was certainly not different. If she really wanted to be different, she would have to study style and create her own unique style. Sue agreed to take lessons in fashion and sewing and is now couture for not only herself, but also the West Villagers of New York who seek out her designs. By the way, her dad's trading is better than ever and he is proud of his daughter and her accomplishments even though he still thinks that some of her choices are "weird."

Life After Life

After Sylvia's mom died, she asked her eighty-five year old dad, Ben, to move in with her family. The unintended consequence of her act of kindness was that his interference in her life created a disaster for her trading. Ben had too much time on his hands and felt depressed because he was no longer productive. He was in Sylvia's hair from morning until night. Sylvia did not want to take advantage of her dad and burden him with household chores and child responsibilities. After all, he had just lost his wife. However, Sylvia had a career, a house to manage, two children and a husband. With the added stress of having her father underfoot, she found it difficult to concentrate on her trading.

Now, Sylvia's dad is an asset rather than a liability. Sylvia told him that she really needed his help and gave him a short list of tasks that relieved her from a lot of her daily pressures. Her dad cares for the garden, runs errands and manages Sylvia's office. Ben feels needed and productive and has become an asset to her trading results.

Strategies for Solving Personal Issues

When confronted with personal issues, we have the choice of avoiding them or dealing with them. Avoiding issues is probably the most common way that people deal with them. But, avoidance only makes the issue fester until it is impossible to avoid and it has to be dealt with. Of course, dealing with it then becomes another problem. You can deal with these issues in a negative way where the outcome results in more problems, or you can deal with an issue in a constructive way. Usually, the negative method seems easier because it requires less commitment, less energy and less courage. But, it never pays off, as you will see below.

Common negative strategies people use in handling personal issues:

1. Accumulating negative feelings until there is no choice but to make radical change. This results in traumatic feelings for everyone involved because the relationship is over.

2. Accumulating negative feelings that result in an explosion of emotional outbursts causing bad feelings for all concerned. Temporary changes may result because of fear of ending the relationship, but the anger will erupt again.

3. Handling issues by stating problems through anger, proposing solutions, and agreeing to behavior modifications about which neither party is happy. Resentment builds when this method is used.

Common positive strategies people use in handling personal issues:

1. Handling issues by asking a third party to be a mediator and agreeing to behavior modifications worked out through mediation. Both parties agree to follow the plan without resentment. This follow-through is monitored over a period of time until the behaviors are a natural part of every day life.

2. Handling issues together by stating problems to each other without hostile undertones and coming up with agreeable solutions. Both parties commit to taking action without resentment. The commitment is measurable by completed tasks within a specified period of time. Consequences of not completing tasks are also agreed upon.

Remember, if you do not make a choice, you are automatically making one of the first choices.

Conclusion

Personal issues that are not properly handled can sabotage the best trading systems and the most committed efforts. They cannot be ignored and avoided for long because they create stress and drain precious energy and attention. Sometimes, all it takes to turn a bad situation around is to talk it out with a third party, if necessary, while focusing on meeting everyone's needs. But, it does require that you make choices and commitments, and then follow through.

Chapter 7

_____

TOO GOOD FOR TRADING

Many of the traders with whom I work in private consultation have come from families with major dysfunctions that created major trading problems. It is not a surprise when a dysfunctional family creates problems for a trader. What surprises me is when I find a trader with problems that resulted from a loving and supportive family operating from the best of intentions. Sometimes, even good practices in a family can create sabotage in a trader's bottom line.

No Pain, No Gain

Sam was an only child who was lovingly welcomed into an older couple's life. Sam's father, Dan, was going to make sure his son had all the advantages of a happy life while Sam's mother, Margaret, was going to make sure he was protected and supported.

As a child, Dan worked to support his family through the Depression. He remembered having to get up in the early hours of the morning to deliver newspapers in the freezing cold Boston winter. Dan was determined that his young son would only know pleasure. Both Sam's parents were supportive of Sam's interest in sports. They discouraged him from engaging in activities that would be anything but fun.

Margaret was a traditional, stay-at-home mom who walked Sam to school in the mornings, picked him up promptly at three, and had freshly baked chocolate chip cookies and hot chocolate waiting for him when he returned. In short, Sam's parents made a concerted effort to protect him from every painful experience in life. At one point in his childhood, Sam remembers being bullied by older boys and by one boy, in particular, who took his lunch money. He told his parents what was happening. Suddenly, neither this boy nor any of the other boys ever bothered him again. Sam never found out what his parents had done to make it so. Did the fact that his parents ran interference for him throughout his childhood make Sam a happier and more successful person and trader? Read on.

The Big Bad Markets

Sam went on to get college scholarships and to be a successful executive. However, later on, when he entered the world of trading, he discovered that his parents could not be there to protect him from "the big bad markets." Suddenly, he was on his own and Sam had no idea how to protect himself from the fear of facing entry and exits of the market. "To this day," he told me, " I regret that I didn't fight that bully. I know that I would have gotten beaten up because he was four years older than me, but I would have felt so much better about myself. I needed to do my own fighting even if it meant being beaten up."

Through timeline work Sam was given the experiences he felt he was missing and is now able to face the market with good strategies as his protection.

Good Intentions

Jerry's parents were strict Catholics who were going to make sure that Jerry was a good person in every way. He attended a Catholic school at which a group of determined nuns shared the same goal with his parents. Like all the boys at school, Jerry believed the rumor about "the spanking machine" in Mother Superior's office, which continuously spanked bad boys. To avoid a perpetual spanking, Jerry decided that he would never find himself in her office. His strategy for keeping out of any kind of trouble was to anticipate the needs and wants of the people in his life, and give them what they wanted before they asked. In this way, he would not have to face punishment. For example: he would wash the dishes for his mom before she asked, work hard to get good grades to keep her happy and avoid any behavior that would upset the nuns. This strategy of being good worked for him as a child and throughout college.

The Spanking Machine

Jerry, too, began his career in corporate America, where he applied his strategy of anticipating other's needs. He soon found himself working sixteen-hour days that were never long enough. While his plan pushed him up the ladder of success, Jerry was pulling himself down in the area of health. Eventually, he discovered the world of stocks and eventually went out on his own as a trader and was successful initially.

When Jerry married Ruth, he tried to please her in every way. For his children, he made sure that they wanted for nothing. Unfortunately, both Jerry's wife and children were insatiable. With the pressure of constantly giving more and more to his family Jerry began to get panic attacks that led to depression, which in turn led to bad trading. In the midst of his emotional and financial travails, his wife left with the children.

All the parts of Jerry's life had combined to become one, large spanking machine. He was getting punished from every direction, regardless of the fact that he was trying to be good. Or maybe it was because he was trying so hard to be good to everyone but himself.

When I worked with Jerry, he had already put his life back on track and was healthy, happy, and redefining his business plan for trading. But, low and behold through the business and personal choices he was making for his life, Jerry was setting himself up for another round of the spanking machine. We had to change Jerry's pattern of making the wrong choices before he would be able to trade without sabotage.

Over Cautious

When Neil was born, his father, Arthur, was going to make sure that he would be a healthy baby. Everything in the nursery was white and sterilized daily. No one could visit Neil unless he wore a mask. Despite all of Arthur's efforts to protect Neil from illness, Neil turned out to be a very sickly baby. We now know that a child's immune system will not develop properly unless he is exposed to the germs that kick-start the immune system into action. But, at the time, Arthur was acting out of the very best intentions by keeping him in a sterile environment.

Thus, whenever Neil would catch a cold or get any kind of infection, the doctor was instructed to give him an antibiotic. Throughout his school career, Neil continued to be sick. He was allergic to everything in his environment and suffered from asthma. Somehow, Neil made it through school and college. Having spent a lot of time home sick, he had the time to read his father's Wall Street Journals and fell in love with the markets. Inevitably, he found his way into trading, where he discovered a passion and a talent for the profession.

The problems for Neil in his trading are all the result of his poor health. Instead of having the energy and stamina to trade at the level of his talent and commitment, Neil works at 25% of his capacity. Most of the time, he feels so exhausted that he has a difficult time concentrating or sitting up in his chair. And, what did his doctor recommend, more antibiotics.

After visiting a medical/holistic doctor I recommended, the great irony for Neil was that he was told he harbors a terrible strain of bacteria in his body from excessive antibiotic use. He cannot take more antibiotics to destroy these microorganisms for fear of making matters worse. These bad bacteria are preventing the growth of normal, healthy bacteria in his body, which assist in the digestion of his food and the production of B vitamins needed for countless vital processes. In addition, these bad bacteria release the toxins, which make him feel weak and damage his liver and kidneys. Currently, he is undergoing a treatment, which, hopefully, will bring him to a state of well-being. All this hardship for Neil was a result of the very best of intentions.

Parent Homework

Ronny and Jones' daughter, Stephanie, an exceptionally beautiful girl, would always count on her parents to do or complete her homework. Stephanie did not like school and having to deal with paying attention to lessons. Her parents and teachers agreed that her looks were the asset that would make her successful in the future, so her teachers let her squeak by in getting a high school education. To add to Stephanie's parents good intentions for their daughter she did not learn any domestic skills, because they felt she should be treated like the princess they raised her to be.

Fading Beauty

Stephanie became a model in the Garment District of New York City and married her high school sweet heart, John. He worked for his dad until he graduated with a economics degree from college. John went on to become a trader on the New York Stock Exchange. Stephanie stopped work to have children, did not know how to be a homemaker, gained weight and grew apart from her husband who was expanding his knowledge and horizons in life. John was now a successful trader interacting with interesting educated people. Although John cared for Stephanie, he was embarrassed by her not taking care of herself, their home and making conversation interesting. This began to affect his trading. While Stephanie would have done anything to keep her marriage, she did not have the skills or discipline to know how to pull herself back in shape and transform herself into the person John could be proud of. Arguments between John and Stephanie led to him spending less time at home and more time with friends. At one of the parties John attended, he met a woman who had beauty, grace, domestic skills and education. This resulted in him leaving his wife and eventually getting back on track in being a successful trader.

Mommy & Daddy Dearest

All normal people want the best for their children. Our parents are models for what to do and what not to do in raising us. Even though we try to raise our children to have happy healthy and successful lives, our choices might not be the best for the choices they make later on in life. Here are some examples of choices that could lead to problems with having a trading business:

1. If a child wants to be entrepreneurial and has always seen a steady paycheck coming in, his parents would not have given a good model to be a risk taker.
2. If parents believe that to be happy you should stay within your own values or class, but a person feels he can make lots of money as a trader, he will probably have conflict from his parents' values and values he wants to have for himself.
3. If parents support going into a profession that is considered to be a contribution to the well being of society, but discourage being a trader because it is considered to be gambling, a person wanting to be a trader might find himself feeling guilty going against his parents' best intentions.
4. If parents instill in you the value of security and discourage risk taking, you will probably fear taking a position and hanging on to a good run.
5. If your parents have had a bad experience in risking capital in the markets, they will discourage you because they don't want you to feel the same pain of loss. This might make you apprehensive about trusting yourself as a trader.

Conclusion

Every combination of how we are raised can lead to some form of sabotage in trading results, even if our parents raised us in the most supportive environment. It is important that traders recognize when they are blocking their full potential so that they can take the necessary steps to clear up these issues.

Chapter 8

RUNNING AWAY FROM THE HARD THINGS
PART 1

Recently, I heard about a woman who told her children that whenever they ran away from something that was hard to face, they simultaneously took a giant step away from a happy life. As her children grew up, they hated hearing that same old admonition from their mother, but they took it to heart, nevertheless. And, indeed, they all lead happy lives.

This caveat is especially apt for traders because the things that are hard for us to face are the very things that hold the key to our vulnerabilities. The hard things are often the things that make us uncomfortable, frightened, insecure, incompetent and impatient. They are also the very things that keep us from succeeding.

As one of my oldest and wisest clients always asks, "What does this have to do with making money?" The answer is: everything.

Admitting You are Wrong

For many traders, the hard things involve admitting they are wrong. They cannot find a way to deal with having made a wrong choice, taken a wrong position, or making a mistake. So, they cannot change their minds. And they cannot apologize. The result? Unable to admit they are wrong means that they are stuck on the wrong path, a path that leads to losses and poor results. Unable to apologize means that they are boxed into an emotional corner and forced to defend the indefensible behind a wall of guilt. Without the support of strong relationships, traders have a difficult time dealing with the stress of trading over time.

Taking Time to Plan

For many traders, the hard things involve taking the time to plan. Planning requires the willingness to examine a host of realities that can be uncomfortable. What really are my goals? What really are my resources? What are the obstacles in my path? What steps do

51

I need to take to reach my goals? Am I able, willing and prepared to take those steps? Answering these questions is absolutely essential to the building of a long-term, successful trading business.

Being Disciplined

For many traders, the hard things involve being disciplined. Being disciplined often means saying no to yourself when you want to say yes. It can also mean delaying gratification for a long time. It can mean doing something that is painful. In fact, being disciplined nearly always means doing the hard thing when the easy thing is calling to you. And, as you already know, success in trading requires, above all else, being disciplined.

Being Organized

For a fair number of traders, the hard thing means being organized. These attention-deficit traders want to leap into trading and forget about taking the small and unexciting steps that lay the foundation for an organized business approach to trading. Having rescued a number of traders who were drowning in their own disorder, I can tell you from my experience that to succeed, a trader must be highly organized. He cannot run from this requirement for very long without tripping on his own mess.

Dealing with Money Issues

For some traders, the hard things have to do with money. That fact may seem incongruous for a member of a profession that is all about making money, but it is true, nevertheless. Fear of money and all manner of issues relating to money keep certain traders from dealing with their money management. And what could be more important to keeping your risk in line than dealing with money management?

Dealing with People

For some traders, the hard things have to do with people. Many traders are attracted to trading for the very reason that they do not enjoy working with or relating to others. While their people skills have never been very sharp, their math skills, their analytical skills, and their love of games, research and solving problems have all been exceptional. So, they organize their lives in such a way as to avoid having to deal with people. Unfortunately, a trader who runs away from people is a trader who is running toward trouble. First, a trader needs the support of family and friends to handle the emotional demands of trading. Second, a trader will need to deal with people if he wants to increase his trading capital with other people's money. And third, the business of trading requires a certain amount of interaction with people. That interaction, regardless of how limited, is important in lubricating the wheels of a trader's business.

Dealing with Health Issues

Dealing with health issues is a very hard thing for many traders. Acknowledging the need to take care of their health makes many people feel frightened and vulnerable. They realize, unconsciously, that if you have to be concerned about your health, you are mortal. Since the prospect of their own death is too frightening, unbelievable or unacceptable to deal with, they practice avoidance. Thus, instead of going to the doctor or dentist and the gym in a proactive way that heads off future problems, they stick their heads in the sand and pretend they will live forever. Unfortunately, I know from my experience with traders that the stress demands inherent in trading can lead to serious illness if traders fail to practice healthy and proactive disciplines.

Dealing with Emotions

For many traders, the hardest things involve dealing with their emotional life. These traders can conquer the most difficult intellectual challenges imaginable and find solutions to problems that leave their vanquished fellow traders in their dust. They can work long hours, discipline their bodies and ask strangers for money on the phone. But, they cannot handle their feelings and, therefore, they cannot trade their own brilliant systems.

What Makes Rabbits Run?

John Updike, the great 20th Century American novelist, wrote a series of books about a character named Rabbit, who was fearful of his life's realities. In *Rabbit, Run*, unable to face his life, Rabbit takes to the road only to discover that the realities of escape are just as hard, if not harder, to handle and eventually returns. This odyssey is the story of many traders who run from the hard things and then find that the escape is ultimately more painful than the reality they are fleeing.

So, why do they run in the first place?

1. **Fear**
   The principle reason that traders run from the hard thing is fear. Facing the hard thing usually inspires fear of pain, of loss, of failure, or of humiliation. Most traders would deny that fear is the reason they avoid the hard things. To admit to feeling fear makes traders feel vulnerable and weak. Instead, they will create a host of clever intellectualizations and explanations for their avoidance. The fact remains, however, that fear is the real reason.

2. **Patterns of Behaving**
   Once an individual associates pain with a particular issue or experience, he develops a coping mechanism. Running away and avoiding are very successful coping mechanisms for protecting yourself from experiencing pain. After all, our species would not have survived nearly four million years on this planet without good survival mechanisms. The first time you successfully run from the hard thing, you

feel a rush of relief. "Whew! That was close." Now, in your unconscious mind, this feeling of relief is interpreted as a reward for taking the right step. In the future, when faced with the same set of circumstances and the same feeling of fear and discomfort, you will have a "Plan A" response that is guaranteed to bring relief. After a few more encounters with the hard thing, you will have an ingrained pattern of responding.

3. **Lack of Immediate Negative Consequence** – Anyone who has ever tried to train a dog finds out that you cannot punish him a day after he chewed on the furniture and make an impact on his behavior. Running from the hard thing rarely has an immediate consequence either. The consequences of not doing the hard thing usually appear over time and are not linked to the original act of avoidance.

Thus, we run from doing the hard things because of fear and our response becomes a pattern because we do not pay the immediate cost for avoiding a painful or uncomfortable experience. But, down the road, the costs add up.

Conclusion

In "Part 2 of Running Away from the Hard Things" we will look at strategies a trader can use to break the pattern of avoidance. Until then, you can work on the first step in the process. The first step is to simply take a look at the things that you are running away from. What are the things that make you uncomfortable? Examine the feelings you have that make you want to avoid some of the essential issues in your trading business. Write them down. If you have trouble figuring out what you are running from, reread the list of common issues in this article and ask yourself if you avoid dealing with each issue. The Act of acknowledging a problem is often the hardest step, but you cannot reach your goal without taking that first step.

Chapter 9

RUNNING AWAY FROM THE HARD THINGS
PART 2

In Part One of this series, we looked at the problem of running away from the hard things and listed some of the most common issues that make traders take the road to avoidance. Unfortunately, running from hard things eventually affects the bottom line for traders. The operative word in this statement is "eventually." The immediate result of avoidance is instantaneous relief, but the long-term result can mean that the trader not only loses momentum toward achieving his goals, he may never reach his goals at all.

Strategies for Dealing with the Hard Things

Fear is usually the reason that traders run from the hard things. The reason can be fear of failure, fear of pain, fear of embarrassment, fear of discomfort or even fear of boredom. Listed below is a set of strategies that can help you stop running from the hard things and deal them in a way that will take the fear out of them.

1. **Identify the Issue**
   Make a list of things that you run away from. Be honest about what you are avoiding. Write down the things that trigger your avoidance and the specific feelings that you have when confronted with the hard things. In addition, write down the steps you take to avoid dealing with the hard things you avoid.

   Identifying your issues is the first step in gaining control of them. Once you have acknowledged that there is a problem, it has less power over you than when you attempt to conceal it. Furthermore, it is impossible to deal with a problem if you do not know what it is. The more detail you bring to the description of the problem, the more easily you can identify the causes and the negative anchors that you have created.

2. **Create a Hierarchy for your Issues**
   When a Neuro-linguistic programmer works with a fear, he locates the greatest fear

and works down to the least threatening fear. For example, suppose you fear speaking in public. You avoid any and all opportunities to speak in public because you feel as if you would have a heart attack whenever you get up in front of an audience. The problem here is that you could dramatically expand your trading capital pool if you were willing to make presentations to several local groups of investors but your fear makes you unwilling to try

Now, let's create a hierarchy for this issue. Let's suppose that the most frightening thing you could imagine would be to have to stand alone in front of a large and hostile audience and without preparation talk extemporaneously. Your talk would be telecast around the world and your entire future would depend on how well you did. Is that enough pressure to make you want to run? What would be the least threatening public speaking situation for you? Suppose you were to present a brief and carefully rehearsed talk to your dog and cat? Or if your audience cannot be living, how about making a presentation to your video library? Could you do that?

Find a simplified version of the hard thing that you are avoiding that is so unthreatening that you can handle it. Then, do it and move up to the next step and the next, until you are talking to children's groups, and then young adults, and then people who are your peers. One day, you will be speaking in front of audiences without so much as a three by five note card to keep you on track.

3. **Mental Rehearsal**
When a diver is learning to perform a new dive, he or she cannot begin practicing it twenty feet in the air. That height on a narrow diving board is not a good place to make a mistake. Gymnasts and skaters also need to learn new moves where the risk of accident and injury is minimized. They are more likely to learn a move faster, safer and better if it is mentally rehearsed before it is performed on the board, floor, or ice.

If you have never used the process of mental rehearsal, you will be pleased to learn that anyone can do it. All you need to do is visualize yourself doing a particular thing. The trick to successful mental rehearsal is to create as much detail in the mental picture as possible. For the diver who is learning a new dive that requires him to twist his body in a particular way, he can imagine himself on the board, leaping and turning his body in the right way at exactly the right moment and landing in the water perfectly without a splash. In his mind's eye, he can feel the water, hear the sounds of the pool area, smell the chlorine in the water and see every detail around him. Then, just as he would practice this dive in real life, he must continue to rehearse it in his mind.

The same process works for virtually any action that you may be currently avoiding. If you find that you are avoiding the process of organizing your office, imagine yourself doing it in detail. See your office becoming more and more organized as you continue in your visualization. There is an extra variable that you need to include in your mental rehearsals for things that you are avoiding. You must add an emotional component of pleasure, satisfaction, peace, relief, pride, and happiness – all of the good feelings that you are going to experience by taking the plunge and doing the hard things. Each time you rehearse it, you need to build up the positive emotional charge.

After some practice, you will find that you will feel comfortable doing the hard thing in your mind. In fact, you will eventually look forward to doing it. After all, you have done it so many times that it is no longer painful, frightening, boring, awful and unfamiliar.

4. Find a Way to Enjoy the Hard Things

The reason that we avoid the hard things in life is that there is no pleasure in the process, only pain. At least, that is how we have created it in our mind. Neuro-linguistic programming looks at the way that the human mind works and attempts to use the information to improve our lives. One of the keys to the workings of the human mind is how associations are built to nearly everything in our lives.

The reason that we run from the hard things is that we have learned to associate fear, pain and discomfort with them. If we want to find a reason to stop avoiding these things, we must reframe our experience of these hard things. In other words, find a way to enjoy them. Create positive associations.

Suppose that you are a trader who avoids spending time with your wife and children. You have never been comfortable around people and you are even less comfortable around children. As a result, you find it very hard to be with your family for any period of time. You hardly know your children, your wife has withdrawn from you, and you lead parallel, non-intersecting lives. Because of the distance, you get no emotional nourishment or support from your own family.

Now, suppose that you could reframe the experience and see yourself having a great time with your family. One way to accomplish this would be to focus on the things about the family members that you find positive, enjoyable, funny, rewarding – even if these things are trivial compared to the overwhelming feelings of discomfort that you normally feel. If your children seem loud and demanding, think back to moments when they have made you smile and feel proud. Frame the picture of them in your mind at that moment. If reading to them at bedtime is the only time that you have that feels rewarding to you, then extend that time with them. If trips with them are painful, find ways to reduce that pain by planning activities for them en route that are fun and will keep them occupied.

Reframing your associations can change your life. Reframing can turn experiences that you dread into experiences that you look forward to. However, you are responsible for your associations. You made them and in order to change them, you must be willing to devote the necessary time and effort. You might also need to find someone to help you in the process of reframing your associations. The good news is that this process can be done if you are committed to it.

5. Reward Yourself for Doing the Hard Things

Motivation is a key to doing the hard things. Very few mortals are willing to do the hard things just because they are there and need to be done. Most of us need a reason that is powerful enough to help us overcome our reluctance to feel pain, fear or discomfort. One of the most effective ways to overcome reluctance is through a system of rewarding good behavior. Thanks to behavior modification psychologists, we know that humans and lab rats will continue to do things that are painful if they receive the right rewards afterwards.

What are the right rewards? Rewards can represent something different for each of us. Only you know which rewards will make you smile and help you to overcome your reluctance to 'hang in there' when the going is unpleasant. It is important that the rewards be positive ones. Do not fall into the trap of rewarding positive behavior with negative rewards. Negative rewards are rewards that will undermine your best efforts. This could include a drink or food, or a spending spree that you cannot afford, or anything that feeds an addiction.

Examples of positive rewards are:

- Time out to read a book that you are currently reading and have really gotten into
- A message from a professional
- A movie
- A tennis game or game of golf with a friend
- A trip, either a quick inexpensive one or a real blow out—depending on the value to you of doing the hard thing
- An evening alone with no one bothering you for any reason
- A purchase - such as a piece of software for your computer or a new DVD player

Whatever the reward, remember to make it meaningful so that your unconscious mind feels satisfied.

6. Create Consequences

At the same time that you are rewarding yourself for doing the hard thing, it is important to let your unconscious mind feel the pain of not doing it. Since the consequences of not 'doing the hard thing' are rarely immediate, you need to write down the long-term consequences so that you can see what the cost really is to you. It is also important to list the cost to the people who are important to you, as well. Since your family is likely to be affected, the consequences are doubled. For example, if the hard thing is to manage your business and home finances because it makes you deeply anxious, you need to list the consequences to your family if you were to lose everything. By listing the negative consequences, you increase the pain to the point where you become highly motivated to take action to reduce it.

Do not use negative consequences alone to motivate yourself. Once you have enumerated the negative consequences of not doing the hard thing, list the benefits to you and your family of doing the hard thing. For many traders, this list is as much of a revelation as the negative consequences. As you begin to see what you are missing by not doing the hard thing, your level of motivation increases as well. It is important to have both lists to create a balanced view of the situation and to tip the scales in favor of positive action.

7. Have a Partner in the Process

Find someone who will be your partner in the process of doing the hard thing that you avoid. This person needs to be someone who will be a cheerleader and will pat you on the back when you succeed. They also need to be someone who will do the hard things with you and will listen to you when you backslide. The Weight Watchers organization helps people to control their eating by linking them with others who can share the effort through support. There are other support groups around the country for people who are attempting the shed their demons and work on the hard things. For example, there are all of the twelve-step support groups for people with addictions such as Alcoholic's Anonymous, Gambler's Anonymous, and Overeater's Anonymous. Find a support system or simply find a friend who has the same issue and work together to support each other.

8. Model on Success

Find an individual who is doing the hard thing successfully and model on him or her. Make certain that the person you model is not only successful in the area of doing the hard thing you avoid, but is also a person you would want to be like. Would you really want to have his whole life? Decide what parts of your personality are in alignment with the person you want to model and model on them. Modeling is probably the fastest way to learn and make changes in your life.

9. Associate with Winners

Find people who are doing the hard thing consistently and associate with them. This step might include joining a club or association. For example, if the hard thing for you is speaking in public, you might want to join the Toastmasters Club. Or, if the hard thing for you is interacting with people, you might want to join a civic club or an organization like Habitat for Humanity so that you are interacting with others in a constructive and non-threatening way. Without realizing it, you will begin to absorb the ethic of the people who are successfully doing the hard thing. Then, suddenly, you will find yourself doing it, as well.

10. Get Training

Sometimes, the reason that something is painful and difficult is that we really do not know how to do it. What we need is some tutoring or training. Consider going to the library or the bookstore and loading up on books on the subject, or take a course or a seminar. Several years ago, two women whose homes were always a mess and who could not seem to manage the disorder got together and decided to figure out how to overcome their aversion to keeping order. They discovered that they simply did not know how to manage disorder. So, they learned and they wrote a book about it so that they could teach others. If you need to hire a counselor or a coach to help you to learn how to do the hard thing, do it. Find what it takes to give you insight into how to do the hard thing so that it is no longer hard.

11. Create a Plan

Finally, the steps to doing the hard thing derive from your objectives, which come from your goals. If you know what your goals are, they give you the passion and the direction needed to overcome your obstacles along the way. The goals need to be so powerful that they are constantly in your consciousness. Powerful goals create a passion that motivates you past all the hard things. But you cannot do this unless you have taken the time to plan. Although I have listed it last, planning is ultimately your very first step. From it, all things flow naturally. Without it, you are working in circles, duplicating efforts, backtracking, and losing momentum. Take the time to create a comprehensive business and life plan. The hard things will become less hard as a result.

Conclusion

As you can see, there are nearly a dozen highly effective strategies for overcoming your reluctance to do the hard thing. Suddenly, it is no longer so hard and it no longer looms over you like a powerful beast. You have the means to tame it and all you need is the desire and the willingness to do so. Remember that you are not alone in this process. There are countless others who have the same problems and just as many who have a strategy for doing it successfully. Reach out for support and you will find it. Doing the hard thing will one day become an easy thing for you and you will be ready to take the next step in your life.

Chapter 10

THE COURAGE TO BE A TRADER

Trading is not sympathetic to the meek and the mild. Few professions require as much courage as trading does. Most traders do battle from the time they come into the profession until the time they retire. From the initial educational phase, to fighting the negativity of significant people in their life, through the challenge of finding a methodology that works, there always seems to be another hurdle to face. Then, the difficulties of environmental issues, psychological issues and the ever-changing markets must be added to the mix. Each new step that must be taken and each new issue that must be addressed requires courage. The rewards of money, excitement and conquering personal demons are what motivate traders to conquer the next challenge and summon up the requisite bravery.

To understand how much courage it takes to be a trader, let's take the trader's journey and examine the hurdles he must overcome.

Innocence Lost

The first time a trader walks into a trading room and feels the excitement welling up inside, he wants to shout, "I've found it! I found my destiny!" He rushes to the nearest bookstore to buy a book called *Trading for Dummies*, and as soon as he reads it, he places his ten thousand dollars in life savings in a brokerage account and proceeds to lose it all. Our trader has learned his first big lesson and paid his first rite of passage. Each step along the path will require him to pay for his rite of passage with another show of courage.

So, You are Going to be a Gambler...

Our trader's first big loss has knocked him off his horse. Once he dusts himself off and gets back up on the horse, he will have left behind all of the traders who cried "Uncle" and gave up. The next obstacle to confront is all of those wonderful, supportive people in his life who suddenly stop being supportive and fill the air with messages of fear and negativity: "Are you nuts? Do you want to be a gambler like your Uncle Lenny?" They will tell him stories about other sorry fools who took the same path and lost everything. They will urge him to reconsider his career choice for his own sake and for the sake of his wife and children.

Many traders do not have the courage to stand up to this orchestrated barrage of nay-sayers. Trying to convince well-meaning loved ones who do not understand that trading is a viable profession is especially difficult if you do not approach trading as a businessman yourself. Until our trader takes the steps needed to be a professional trader, he will have to proceed without the support of the important people in his life. To gain their support, he will have to demonstrate to them that he has more than the desire to be a trader. He must also have the education, training and experience to succeed.

"Reading, Riting and Rithmatic"

Now, our trader will take his first step on the path of the warrior trader. That first step is education. Not until he takes that first step will he be able to call himself a professional trader. The chances are, however, that at this point, he will realize that he does not have the fortitude to face the hurdles of this dynamic profession. After all, trading books can be very intimidating to the novice and can scare him off. However, he will successfully complete this step if he starts off reading books that are simple and builds on them with progressively more challenging ones.

And yes, our trader must hit the books and read everything he can find about trading and the markets. Without a good foundation in understanding the markets beyond "books for dummies," our trader has nothing to fall back on in the ever-changing markets. If he wants to be a long-term, consistently good moneymaker, he must have an understanding of how to handle anything that the markets will do. Many programs, seminars and coaches are available to the trading public. However, the majority of a trader's education has to come from his own hard-earned experience. It is important to note that this part of the journey never stops. While the educational part of the journey becomes less of a hurdle the more he reads, our trader can be caught unaware if he does not continue to educate himself throughout his career.

Why do I Need a Plan? It's Just Trading.

Once our trader has built a foundation in knowledge, the next hurdle is putting it all together in a business plan. After twelve years as a Traders' Coach, it is still amazing to learn how many so-called professional traders do not have a written business plan. And it must be written down. Our trader will find that by doing so he will organize his business and find the flaws in his methodology. This effort will save him from learning a lot of lessons through losses. Many traders do not want to fill out a business plan because they want to trade by the seat of their pants. They find it boring and stifling to trade by written rules. In my experience, the best traders are those who are discretionary, using an intuitive indicator. Until our trader has a method that he can write down with definitive

66

rules, he cannot rely on his method. And, yes, intuition can be quantifiable and reliable when monitored over a period of time. In fact, I believe it is the most reliable indicator a trader has as long as he has put his physical, emotional and mental states into balance.

Testing, Testing and MoreTesting

Within our trader's business plan is his methodology. While the past does not equal the future, he needs the confidence that comes from believing that he can achieve a successful outcome in order to reach his goals. The best way to build that confidence is to test his methodology. As he tests his system using several different methods, it is likely that he will discover that his method is not reliable. So, he adjusts the parameters to fit the current state of the market and his methodology works fine until the market changes. Suddenly, his system is telling him that he is wrong. The stress resulting from each adjustment leads to emotional upheaval. Our trader finds himself throwing tantrums out of frustration, fear and anger.

Once again, our trader faces another rite of passage. Not only is his methodology being tested but his own courage to succeed is being tested as well. At this point, he either works through his temper tantrums or he abandons trading. Suddenly, he realizes that tantrums or rather the lack of them separates the die-hard trader from the traders who cannot make the grade.

Begging, Borrowing and Saving

Just as our trader has begun to believe that he can now be a money-making machine, he is faced with another hurdle to overcome. He discovers that he should have been accumulating monetary resources specifically for his trading capital. His trading money can only represent a very small part of his family's savings, because he does not want to make himself vulnerable to financial ruin on the way to becoming a trader. Using family savings will add stress to him and his family. If he does not have enough money to be in the trading business, he should only trade part-time until he can trade free of the stress of financial pressure.

Starting and maintaining a trading business requires capital beyond the money our trader needs to trade. The average good trader earns 20% on a consistent basis. If our trader calculates his living expenses, his cost of doing business and what capital he has to trade, the sum is a good indicator of his readiness to enter the profession on a full-time basis. While there are those exceptional traders who earn very high percentages, the majority of traders do not. Our trader can consider it a triumph to be counted among those traders who are just average. They may be average traders, but they are certainly not average people. It is a tremendous accomplishment to have conquered the obstacles in the path to becoming a trader.

Computer and Trench Warfare

The big day has arrived for our trader who is ready to take his first trade as a professional. He thinks he has acquired excellent equipment, a good data service, and fast connections through his local cable company. However, obstacles are still lying in wait along the way:

- his computer dies for no apparent reason
- his computer is running but he has data service outages
- he has trouble getting stock splits in a timely way in the data base
- it takes days for his operation to get back into full service

Does our trader continue to beat on his computer and rant at anyone who will listen, or has he learned to live with the frustrations like most traders? Even when everything goes smoothly, he still faces the problems of getting fast fills with little slippage. As a professional trader, all these things encompass his trading environment. If he is surrounded by these problems, he can get upset to the point of not being able to function for the rest of the day. Or he can have the emotional fortitude necessary to learn to take the day-to-day obstacles in stride as part of trading and be stress free and ready to trade when all system are functioning.

Can't Follow the Rules

By now our trader has learned that throwing the computer out of the window creates more delays and that yelling at people just upsets him. Once he is able to work within the framework of what he can do, he must face the biggest obstacle of all: he cannot follow his rules, he cannot pull the trigger, and when he does pull the trigger, he does not exit at the right time. What our trader forgot to include in his foundation was the psychology of trading.

Yes, the psychology of trading exists. Even if a trader is currently making money in his trading, he will sabotage his results if he is not willing to handle his psychological issues. The traders who understand the importance of handling psychological problems before they start trading have a head start on those traders who find out about their issues when they sabotage their trading results. The most common reason that traders avoid dealing with their psychological issues is fear. It takes courage to overcome this trading obstacle.

The Changing Markets

Our trader has finally handled many of his psychological issues and is now a steady, good trader. In the process, he has mastered the flow and rhythm of the market so that he can count on putting money in the bank every month. His parents regard him with pride and call him, "My son the trader." Then, the markets do a flip-flop and the big trends disappear. Now the Bear reigns, but he is still the Bull trader. So, he returns to the drawing board to adjust and accommodate because he is a professional trader who has not lost his passion. As he fights to recover his control, he recognizes the fact that part of being a successful trader is the ability to adapt to these adjustments by learning how to handle stress. The world changes and he must, too. Yet, for a professional trader, these changes are part of the excitement that keeps him going.

Conclusion

Successful, long-term trading is not for the feint of heart. Each step along the way provides challenges to your grit, stamina, flexibility and character: frustrations are an every day event, change is always around the corner, and your own psychology may be sabotaging all of your efforts. Surviving as a professional trader requires the courage to see these obstacles as merely the elements of the game, so that you can play your hand to win.

SECTION 3
Sabotage Traps to Avoid

Chapter 11

_____

LIFE ON HOLD:
PUTTING YOURSELF IN THE TRADING PICTURE

If you have put your trading on hold, you undoubtedly have a compelling reason. To support your case for being stuck, you can find countless others who will nod in agreement and understanding as they wait to tell you their own sad tale. On the other hand, there are traders whose "road-block" stories are just as compelling as yours, but who are successfully trading. Let's look at how traders have overcome their excuses.

No Money

As a new money manager, Joe had only two hundred fifty thousand dollars to manage. His own operating funds were based on a standard fee of 2% of capital and 20% of the 54% profit that he was earning for his clients. Despite his outstanding track record, the income from his business was barely $20,000 a year. After paying his expenses, Joe was living from hand to mouth. Deeply frustrated, he only had enough funds in his bank account for six more months of trading operations. Understandably, his financial situation started to affect his trading profits.

Joe's good reasons for being unable to succeed were:

- insufficient capital
- having no one to market his success as a money manager
- lacking the time or ability to market himself

Tim could have been in a similar situation if it had not been for the fact that he had learned how to market, sell, speak and write on his way to becoming a money manager. Through Toastmasters, he had learned to speak before groups about trading. In the course of reading books for his Toastmasters' speeches, he had also learned about selling and marketing. These books directed him to write articles and to seek out public venues for his ideas. While studying marketing at a seminar, Tim met David who became his marketing and sales representative. In less than the amount of time it took Joe to fail, Tim found his trading firm managing ten million dollars.

Legal Bureaucracy

Recently, I have been hearing about dramatic court cases from traders that have caused them a great deal of stress and delay. A few of these traders have stopped trading while others are fighting daily to sustain their trading performance. These cases cover the gamut from settlements of marriage, child custody, and inheritance battles to business related issues. Here is one example of a legal battle that created havoc in a trader's performance and the strategy that took him off hold.

Jerry owned a building where he leased office spaces. Without his permission, one of his tenants decided to erect a structure on the roof of his building to store a large piece of equipment. This construction project was undertaken without consulting Jerry and without compensating him. Before taking legal action, Jerry asked his tenant to remove the structure and repair the roof. When his request was refused, Jerry was forced to go to court. Now, he has been fighting the legal system for over a year. Like many other traders in his situation, the worry and stress of fighting the system had caused Jerry's health to suffer, as well. He would wake up feeling exhausted and suffered through one illness after another. In the meantime, Jerry's trading has been on hold because of worry, frustration and anger.

When Jerry called for help, I asked him if he was doing everything in his power to resolve the situation. After reciting a short list of tasks he needed to complete, he admitted that the rest was up to his lawyer. "Do you trust your lawyer's ability to handle his part of the job?" I asked him. Jerry assured me that he did. Except to pray, Jerry could take no further actions that were ethical. I asked him what he would do if the case decided against him, what he would do if he had to settle the case, and what he would do if the ruling was in his favor. I instructed Jerry to mentally rehearse each of these scenarios, picturing himself handling each situation with the best possible outcome. Finally, I instructed him to repeat this mental rehearsal every time he began to worry. This exercise helped Jerry to get back on track with his trading.

Changing the Combination

Traders often put their trading on hold when their personal lives go out of kilter. Changes in a trader's marriage and home life take his focus away from his trading.

Sally was Marty's childhood sweetheart. Their marriage was what I call a match made in tribal culture. In other words, Sally and Marty were raised in the same city and shared the same ethnic heritage with its unique values and mores. Thus, their marriage was stable and their lives together was conventional and predictable. Sally became a devoted wife, the perfect homemaker, and the nurturing mother who supported her husband through college and through the growth of his business. Marty became an extremely successful trader. For twenty years, Sally and Marty felt blessed with their relationship.

Even when the demands of his career caused him to neglect his family, Sally stood by Marty and supported his dreams.

Then, along came Liz. Marty thought that he had everything until he met Liz on a business trip. Filled with passion, Liz lit up the room for Marty. Within two months, Marty was hopelessly sucked into the feelings that he had never felt before. He announced to his wife that he was divorcing her. This situation was devastatingly painful for Sally, the children, and even for Marty. Suddenly, the balance that had sustained Marty's life had shifted.

Trading on Hold

While Liz still provides Marty with the passion that he has never known before, the transformation in his life has taken a toll on his trading. The combination of Marty and Sally created a unique chemistry that supported exceptional trading. Now, the new combination of Marty and Liz has placed his trading on hold. Liz makes demands on Marty that drain his mental focus and energy away from trading. Sensing a lack of stability and balance, Marty's clients are withdrawing their capital. His partner, who believes that Marty is out of control, is forced to pick up the ball that Marty has dropped. To make matters worse, Marty refuses to admit that anything is wrong. But, unless he changes the combination, Marty will suffer the consequences. If Marty attempts to change the combination he has with Liz to get his trading back on track, will he end up with the same situation that he had with his wife, Sally?

Life's Issues are Good Reasons to Hold You Back

Robert hated being an engineer and dreamed of being a trader. However, every influence in his life seemed to take precedence over the realization of his dream. The result was that trading was on perpetual hold. The first obstacle was his wife who, afraid of not receiving a paycheck, discouraged her husband's trading. No sooner had they separated than Robert's father took ill. Robert decided to live with his father during his remaining days.

In the meantime, Robert's sister, Sarah, entered the picture. Sarah, who received a house and a new car from her father when she married, neither visited him nor offered to help with his care. When Sarah heard that she was not included in the will, she contested her father's bequest of his house and small bank account to Robert. Again, Robert put his trading on hold while he waited for the court to settle the dispute.

Certainly, Robert had a series of compelling reasons for not following his heart's desire. However, when I asked Robert if he were prepared to trade after the court decision, he related a series of steps that had to take place before he could feel comfortable in leaving his job. I smelled sabotage. I asked Robert what it would take for him to take those steps now. He replied, "My making the decision to do them." Robert made the decision and was prepared to trade when the court case was over.

In Robert's case, he just needed permission from someone else to follow his dreams. It had never occurred to him to give himself permission to proceed. Part of Robert believed that there would be another crises to handle, so why bother? Fortunately, no immediate crisis arose and now he is a happy trader. But, if there had been another crisis, Robert would have put his trading on hold once again.

My Way by Myself

One of the most common reasons that traders put their trading on hold is fear: fear of making a serious mistake, of not being perfect, of failing, of losing face, of losing all of their capital, and of feeling pain. In each case, the fear is of some kind of loss, and loss always results in pain. Better to put their trading on hold, they reason unconsciously, than to deal with the pain of loss.

Gerard was a top executive with a wife and children—or as Zorba the Greek would say, "The Full Catastrophe." After his life situation changed, Gerard decided that he would take early retirement and live his life for himself and do whatever pleased him. One of his dreams was to become a day trader. With books and computers in place, he was on his way. Gerard put together a discretionary day trading system based on a technical foundation, but found it too difficult to take the trades. He did not trust his system and he did not trust himself. Being a perfectionist, he was afraid his interpretation of market opportunities would be wrong. He was also afraid that he would not get the most out of each trade. When he attended my *Trading on Target* Seminar, he learned the importance of filling out a business plan. In front of the seminar group, he made a commitment to complete the business plan that was included in the notes of the seminar. The other major lesson that he learned from the seminar was that he was wrong to not take a trade when his system gave him a signal to do so. By not taking the trade, he was not following his rules as a trader. It was clear that Gerard needed another interpretation of what it means to be wrong in trading.

Gerard is still stuck. He failed to fulfill his commitment to complete a business plan and he has refused to reinterpret the meaning of being wrong. Still trying to trade his own way, Gerard needs to continue to be right. Guess what? He still cannot pull the trigger.

"If you do what you have always done you will get what you have always gotten."

Getting Off Being on Hold

Here is a strategy for pulling yourself out of an emotional sand trap:

1. Recognize that you are stuck and unable to get where you want to be.
2. Verbalize the forces that you believe are responsible for holding you back.
3. Determine what you could do to make a difference in getting what you want.
4. Find your options if what is holding you back is no longer an issue.
5. Find how you could prepare yourself for each possible outcome.

6. Determine if you have to give something up in order to get what you want. Are you willing to do it?
7. Write out a list of everything you must consider in order to reach your goals. Accomplish everything that you can on your own.
8. Consider how to prepare yourself for life after you have attained your goals.
9. If the outcome is assured and you need only wait for it to happen, make the most of that waiting time. Use it to make decisions based upon a positive outcome for you.
10. If you cannot overcome your issues on your own, hire someone who can help you handle them. Hire the best professionals you can afford to help you through this process and let them know the outcome you want.
11. Try to save money during this time to give yourself a safety net. Put money aside each month regardless of whether things are going well or badly for you.
12. After you have taken these initial steps, complete your plan by setting a timeline for the completion of your tasks and develop a contingency plan for everything that can go wrong and everything that can go right. For each contingency, you should develop and rehearse a course of action in response to it.

Conclusion

When stable conditions suddenly change in a trader's life, he often puts his trading and his personal life on hold. Unfortunately, "on hold" can become a permanent state unless he concrete steps are taken to bring order and stability back into his life. For other traders, anything can provide an excuse to put trading on hold. Trading itself may be so great a challenge that a trader may need to examine his beliefs about himself and what he really wants. The process of getting off hold, regardless of the reasons, requires a significant infusion of new energy and commitment and finding this new fount of strength will require that he dig deep inside. He may also need to reach out for help.

Chapter 12

NEVER ENOUGH

Jack is never satisfied with his trading results. Sometimes, he looks to his system for the problem, but no matter how much tweaking he does, the indicators are not quite right. Sometimes, he feels that he is not getting enough timely information no matter how many services, newsletters, and information sources he has. Most often, the problem is simply that, no matter how much money he is making, it is never enough.

Jack is never satisfied with his trading. As a result, he is often frustrated, angry, or depressed. These negative emotions affect his trading so that he rarely trades at the top of his form. If he could feel that he had enough in his life, Jack would trade so well that he would actually make more money in his trading than he had set as a goal for himself.

The Cup-is-Never-Full Syndrome

Of course, Jack is not alone. Many traders experience this sense of never having enough. Their cup is never full regardless of how much life pours into it.

Regardless of how much--
- Praise they receive - they still feel unappreciated.
- Love they receive - they still feel unloved.
- Success they achieve - they are never successful enough.
- Money they make - it is never enough.
- Time they devote to their trading - they still feel that they are not doing enough.
- Security they have - they still feel vulnerable.
- Physical attractiveness they possess - they still feel unappealing.
- Attention they receive - they still feel ignored.

For each individual trader the issues may be different, but the underlying problem is the same.

If a trader were a cup, that cup would need to be completely filled to trade to a level of peak performance. However, this level cannot be achieved if there is a hole in the cup or if the cup is so poorly constructed that it is constantly in need of repair. Unfortunately, many people fall into this category. From their childhood, they possess a legacy of emotional and physical scars that have damaged their vessels so that they leak out whatever is put into them. The result is that their cup is never full, they never have enough, and no matter how hard they try, they cannot achieve their trading goals to their satisfaction.

The Cost of Never Having Enough

Lil called me for help for her husband, Marvin. He did not feel that he needed any help and became angry at Lil for betraying their relationship. According to Lil, Marvin's trading had been in the doldrums for some time. He had an explosive temper that erupted occasionally after periods of relative calm. What frustrated Lil the most was the fact that Marvin seemed to require excessive amounts of praise and displays of gratitude. No matter how much reassurance Lil gave him, Marvin never seemed to be satisfied. If Marvin remembered to empty the trash, it required notice and repeated "Thank You's" because Marvin usually did not hear until after the second or third time.

The effort to fill Marvin's cup became staggering over time. Eventually, Lil would get tired of constantly supporting Marvin and slow the continuous stream to a trickle, occasionally stopping the stream of support altogether. This cessation would result in raging episodes from Marvin that terrified his poor wife.

Marvin's trading was a perfect reflection of his need for reassurance. When Lil was able to give Marvin enough reassurance to keep his cup half-full, he was able to trade adequately. When she gave up or backed off, Marvin became resentful, angry, and unable to trade.

The first cost to Marvin for not being able to get enough reassurance in his life was in his professional life. He was unable to achieve the trading success that his level of commitment, skill, and intelligence should warrant. The second cost to Marvin was in his personal life. Lil's "Thank-You's" and compliments were coming from a place of unnaturalness to her and Marvin was beginning to feel it and react to it in a negative way.

Getting to the Root of the Problem

Both of our traders had childhoods that were directed by critical parents who could never be satisfied. Jack's parents were hypercritical of his efforts in school. If Jack came home with an A minus, he would be scolded for not trying hard enough. If he had an assignment to do a report, he was taken to the library and left all weekend to make certain that he looked up every resource. He was not allowed to go to bed until he had done every chore. Then, once in bed, something was always found that Jack had forgotten to do.

For Jack, the result of this early training was that he came to believe that he had to be perfect in order to be worthy. He could never do well enough unless he had all of the facts and information that he needed. Consequently, he worked tirelessly on his system, he subscribed to all of the information services, and he never felt ready to trade because he knew that he would never be good enough.

Marvin's parents played the same game, but with different results. Nothing Marvin ever did was good enough. While his parents withheld praise and support from him, they were effusive in their praise of his younger sister for everything she did. Marvin came away from this experience filled with rage. Because his experience was connected to his sister as well as his mother, his relationships with women were warped by this early rejection. As a result, he needed constant reassurance and support from his wife and became enraged when she was unable or unwilling to provide it. Of course, it was never enough.

Never Enough

The emotional wounds from one area of life will eventually show up later in the same area or in another area in which there will never be enough.

For example:
- If a trader came from poverty that prevented him from developing a healthy sense of security, he will develop poverty consciousness and there will never be enough money. Prosperity will always elude him. He will find ways to spend his money so there is none left. He will always focus on the pennies and not on the dollars.
- If a trader has been criticized in the past so that his self-esteem is unable to develop properly, like Marvin, he will never be able to get enough compliments. Or, conversely, if he is complimented, he will block them out and not be able to hear them.
- If a young trader is not loved, he will not develop self-love and all the love that will come to him from his family and friends will never be enough. Although he will desperately need to feel loved, he will push those who love him away.
- If all of his accomplishments are criticized, his best results in the market will never be good enough to bring him a sense of accomplishment.

The stress of never having enough will begin to tell on a trader's results and he will start losing money.

What To Do?

Getting professional help is the only way to get the maximum outcome for someone who never has enough. The emotional blockages that cause these patterns of behavior are deeply rooted, but are easily resolved through psychological counseling. That being said, many traders will struggle on, sabotaging their efforts, rather than seeking professional help. However, the following self-help strategy can be employed to reduce many of the drawbacks to the feeling that you can never get enough.

1. First, acknowledge the fact that you are never satisfied with what you get from your world, whether it is from your trading, from yourself, or from others. Determine what you can never get enough of—recognition, praise, love, help, reassurance, validation, money, security, and success.

2. Once you tell yourself what it is that you need, you must give it to yourself. For example, if you feel that you can never have enough praise, give praise to yourself. Do not depend upon others to give it to you. Recognize that when you give praise to yourself, you deserve it even if it may feel uncomfortable. Do it until you are comfortable with it. Soon, you will begin to see a change in your thinking.

3. Tell others what it is that you need. You might want to limit this dialogue at first to those people who care about you. For example: "I need you to let me know when I have done something nice for you that you appreciate it. This is very important to me."

4. Remind the significant others around you that you need to have this reinforcement on a regular basis.

5. Let them know in what form it is the most meaningful to you. Be aware that it might not come to you in the form you expect and be willing to accept it as it comes. For example, you may want to get the expressions of appreciation you need in the form of words: "Thank you so much for what you did. It was really great of you." However, you might get this same result from looks, from gifts, from hugs, or other venues. They mean the same thing. (In the case of Marvin, words were not enough. He needed a hug or some form of touch to accompany the compliment.)

6. When you have been given the thing that you cannot get enough of, acknowledge the fact to yourself and acknowledge to yourself how it made you feel. "My wife just told me how much she appreciates what I did for her and it makes me feel good about myself to hear her say that." Notice if anything is missing.

Although this exercise will not heal the underlying wound, it will reduce your insatiable need for the thing that you cannot get enough of.

Conclusion

A trader who cannot get enough will sabotage his trading results. The unhealed emotional wounds from childhood find a way of expressing themselves in our trading and personal lives so that we feel that we can never have what we want. Although the best way to address these underlying problems is by working with a professional counselor, traders can gain control by acknowledging the problem, openly expressing their needs, and consciously acknowledging their feelings.

Chapter 13

———

LOSING SIGHT OF TRADING AND LIFE

People who choose trading as a career are by nature passionate risk takers in their business and personal life. But what happens when a dream becomes a day-to-day habit and/or a predictable ritual? Will there be a part of you that wants to stir up the old you and in the process sabotage your trading and your life? Or, can you actively do something that keeps the momentum of interest and passion alive?

A Trader is Born

First, there comes the dream of becoming a trader with its trappings of freedom, independence, excitement, and opportunity. Then, comes the process of becoming a trader. For many individuals who are in it for the long haul, the momentum that arrives with the dream carries them through this developmental and growth time with equal excitement. For those who survive this arduous journey and conquer its hurdles, the dream becomes a reality. As a trader, you enjoy the fruits of your labor. But, for some, somewhere along the way, trading becomes boring.

Your Trading

It starts out with the passion of your first true love. You spend fifteen hours a day for two years developing your first trading system. After all of the work and then trial and error testing, the system is refined to the level of a great economic machine. You trade the system successfully for a decade – first with passion, then commitment, then true grit that gets you through the boredom and monotony. Now, you want to do anything, but trade. This afternoon, cleaning swimming pools in Miami sounds good to you as a diversion.

Meeting Your Soul Mate

You meet your soul mate and find yourself flying on new wings. Your thoughts are obsessed with this wonderful person and your level of passion is at its highest. Three years after you marry your soul mate, you discover that your life is routine. Admittedly, it is a good routine, but the sense of discovery and passion is gone. Then, as time passes, the routine becomes stale and you find yourself picking at all of the things that are wrong with the very person that you once defined as perfect.

Children

Your first child is born and you are overwhelmed with a sense of awe. By the time the third child arrives, your awe has turned into "Aw, shucks, how are we going to survive another night without sleep?" The passion that you had for your children has turned into a passion for getting rest and for finding a way to escape the constant noise while trying to figure out a way to pay for their education.

The Hobby

Tennis has become your life's passion. You live for the next French Open and Wimbledon Tournaments. You have your own private tennis coach and you play at least five times a week. Somewhere along the way, your passion for tennis fades and you find that you need a new hobby.

Health

One day, you discover the joy of working out at your local Gold's Gym with some friends. As the years go by, you are a self-proclaimed health nut who takes supplements, engages in good health practices, and reads every health book that you can find. Then, one day you find yourself at McDonald's eating a Big Mac with super-sized french fries and a strawberry shake. You are officially bored with your health regimen.

Routines

A good routine is the original double-edged sword. It is very difficult to accomplish a great deal in a short period of time if you have not established good routines. Without a routine, you are reinventing the wheel each time you perform the same task. This situation will become a routine, in and of itself, if it goes on long enough,

Like driving, there are some things that you need to do automatically and unconsciously in order to accomplish other things. If you have a routine for opening your mail, sorting it, and taking care of it, you can answer the phone and conduct an important conversation at the same time. All of this is good and helpful in the completion of your daily chores.

The problem is that anything that you see all of the time eventually becomes invisible to you. This conditioning is just like anything that you stop smelling because you smell it all of the time and any noise that you stop hearing because you hear it all of the time. Once the things that are important in our lives become routine, we stop noticing them. They become mundane and we tend to lose our passion for them.

In order to keep our passion for something that is important to us, we need to reinvent it on a regular basis.

David Whyte, the Yorkshire-born poet and Fortune 500 consultant, was spurred by a great ambition as a young man to follow in the steps of Cousteau and become a naturalist. With great passion and years of study behind him, he made his way to the Galapagos Islands where he set about in the realization of his dream. But, in his own words, "Every path, no matter how diligently we follow it, can lead to staleness and ennui….our storied islands can seem like a gilded cage…walls that once served and sheltered us at certain periods in our life only imprison us when we have remained within our confines for too long." And, so, he eventually left the islands of his dreams and moved on in his life, reinventing himself.

Reinvention for Traders

The trick for a trader is how to reinvent himself and his trading so that he can continue to enjoy his trading before the ennui becomes so great that he feels that he needs to chuck it all.

1. The first step in the process of reinvention is simply to recognize the challenge. Recognize the potential for boredom and the need to create positive change. If it goes on long enough, acknowledge the fact that you may already be feeling bored and under-stimulated.

2. The next step is to give yourself the room and the freedom to make the necessary changes. You have to make it okay to be creative and to make changes before you can actually do it. You can do this by rewarding yourself for each new step that you take. For example, when you are at your favorite restaurant and want to order the same thing you always eat, order something different and congratulate yourself out loud. Take the time to appreciate the new taste sensations and find enjoyment in them. Keep pushing the envelope.

3. The third step is to make some creative changes in your living environment. When was the last time you rearranged the furniture in your office, in your bedroom, or in your living room? Putting a new painting on the wall can suddenly change the entire feeling of a room. Small changes are often better than major changes because small changes can create big rewards without creating big problems.

4. Ask yourself questions that you do not verbalize normally. For example, "What would make this business more fun?" or "If it didn't matter what the outcome was and it could be easily reversed, what would I like to do with my trading that I'm afraid to do now?" or "What do I miss doing and how could I incorporate that into my work or my life?"

5. Take the time to watch a funny and inventive movie, a science fiction movie, a story that is fantastic or one that challenges your view of life, such as "The Sixth Sense."

Read about subjects that you normally do not explore such as science, history or crime detection. The purpose of this exercise is to get your mind to see your surroundings in a new way so that you can change your paradigm.

Conclusion

This ongoing process of re-imagining and re-revitalizing your trading will allow you to continue to stay in the field, to enjoy the process, and to increase your level of success. David Whyte tells us, "Often, in order to stay alive, we have to *unmake* a living in order to get back to living the life we wanted for ourselves. It is this cycle of making, disintegration, and remaking that is the hallmark of creative and meaningful work."

Chapter 14

MIDLIFE TRADING

When Jack went through his midlife crisis, his trading folded up like a paper umbrella in a pina colada. After a decade of planning out every detail and every contingency of his trading career, he was totally unprepared for the emotional hit he would take when he reached middle age. He had been a highly successful trader - a bona fide market genius. Then, suddenly, before he knew what was happening, he was unable to trade. What happened?

Time Running Out

In Jack's case, what happened was the sudden death of his mother. Although Jack had loved his mother dearly and owed her a great debt of gratitude for all that she had sacrificed to send him to the best schools, he actually spent very little time with her. In fact, in the past decade, as he built his trading business and raised his young family, he had only seen her three times a year, at major holidays. Each Saturday morning, Jack's mother had dutifully called long-distance to check in on him and the grandchildren. In recent times, too busy to talk to her, Jack had put his wife and children on the phone for him. To make matters worse, he had neglected to remember her birthday for the past two years. Fortunately, his wife had remembered at the last minute and arranged for flowers to be delivered to her home. Of course, Jack's neglect had extended to his father, as well, not to mention the rest of his family.

In Jack's mind, his parents were still the strong, independent and eternally young figures of his childhood. They could not age or grow frail because he was still so vital himself. They would be there forever because he wanted it to be that way.

But, Jack had reached midlife, and by extension his parents had reached old age. Time had run out for Jack's mother and this sudden awareness that time was passing by hit Jack very hard.

A Sign of the Times

There are other signs of time running out that bring traders to their knees – literally. For Ed, the sign of the times was when his legs gave out while he was trading in the pit. He fell and his fellow traders rushed to fill in the hole where he had been standing, leaving him virtually helpless to get back up on his feet. Afterward, while his wife was driving him to his palatial suburban Chicago home in their fifty thousand-dollar SUV, it occurred to Ed that he would have done exactly the same thing to a fellow trader just a few years ago.

Ed's doctor informed him that he needed knee surgery, which would require a period of recuperation and physical therapy. Ed was astonished. He had never been sick or injured. He had always considered himself immune to physical problems and limitations, which he associated with old age. Suddenly, he was being placed in that same category. As a result of his injury, Ed was forced to stop trading in the pit for several months. Once he returned, however, his trading was never again as strong as it had once been.

Slipping Through Your Fingers

Midlife crisis hit Rex in an entirely different way. One day, he woke up to see a hairline that had backtracked and a waistline that had expanded overnight. How had he missed the signs? That same morning, he also noticed that his wife had gained weight and was dying her hair. Her conversation, once a source of fascination for him, was painfully predictable. Then, the kids came to the table with a cacophony of complaining and demanding utterings that barely passed for language. From what netherworld had they come?

Suddenly, Rex was asking himself, "Is this all there is?" And before he knew it, Rex was driving a sports car, working out at the gym, and playing around with a young woman named Heather whom he met at a local traders' watering hole. Along with his family, eventually Rex also lost his trading edge.

What's it all About?

For Arthur, a currency trader extraordinaire, the midlife crisis came on a day that he was doing exactly the same things he did every other day. He was going through his mail, organizing and paying his bills, putting together his to-do list for the week, and checking over some of the figures he was using to update his buy charts. A call came from a friend with whom he had not spoken for a very long time. His friend, Michael, was excited because he had just decided to leave his job of twenty years as an engineer and go to Divinity School. Of all people, Mike had gotten the calling! Arthur was flabbergasted. "So, what are you up to these days?" Mike had asked. At that moment, the bottom fell out of Arthur's life. The truth was that he no longer knew the answer to that question.

As the weeks passed, Arthur became obsessed with that question. He looked around at his beautiful and organized life and could not remember what he had found so wonderful about it. What was the meaning of his life? Arthur started seeing a therapist, attending church for the first time in many years, reading the Bible and books on philosophy, religion and spiritual practices. In the meantime, his wife began to panic. What was happening to Arthur? Was he having a nervous breakdown? Since he had stopped trading completely, would they lose everything they had?

What is Happening?

As we reach midlife, we are not prepared for the idea that time can run out on us, or for the startling truth that if we do not hurry to pursue our own definition of a meaningful existence, life can become a repetition of trivial maintenance duties.

When traders have not taken the time to figure out what is truly important to them; they are far more likely to be sucked into the tempest of a midlife crisis. For example, when Jack's mother died, he was shocked by the loss. He was also overwhelmed with guilt and fear. Had Jack been paying attention to the things in his life that were very important, he would have noticed that his mother had been ailing for a long time. He would have seen how tired she was and how frail. So, he would have realized that she was aging along with him. Furthermore, he would have realized that time was passing so swiftly for her that he needed to spend time with her.

Her passing would still have been painful, but it would not have put Jack into a tailspin. He would have continued to trade because he would have been able to take solace in his work.

In the case of Ed, a trader in the pits is dependent upon his physical vitality. Had Ed been paying attention to what was important in his life, he would have realized that he was putting a great deal of strain on his legs every day. He would have taken the time to work out and eat better. As a result, he would also have felt considerably better than he did. In fact, Ed had been suffering from headaches for years. His strategy for dealing with the messages his body was giving him was to take a stronger and stronger headache medicine to cover up the pain. Instead of feeling old, Ed would still be feeling young and vital. And he would still be trading well.

What about Rex? How did he miss the fact that he was getting older? What had he been paying attention to, anyway? Rex had been so focused on the bottom line that he had failed to notice all the lines that were forming above it. Like Jack, Rex had neglected his family for his work. But, unlike Jack, Rex did not receive a wake-up call in time. Instead, he traded his family for a lifestyle that made him feel young again temporarily. The problem with this strategy is that it nearly always backfires. The young and nubile replacement is often more demanding and far less appreciative. In Rex's case, his new girlfriend soon left him for a more attractive sugar daddy. Since Rex's wife and children were so horrified and hurt by his behavior, he is no longer welcome in his old home. Rex's midlife crisis has turned into a nightmare for him.

Rex had spent the first half of his productive years trying to feel good about himself. The principle source of his self-esteem had been how much money he was making in his trading. Suddenly, he realized that how old he looked and how much he was appreciated by others were also important to his self-esteem. Although he woke up to the fact that the sands of time were racing to the bottom, he failed to take the time to dig any deeper into what a constituted a meaningful existence for him.

Arthur, on the other hand, hit midlife crisis with the awareness that he did not know what constituted a meaningful existence. The result was that he was forced to take time out to figure it out. In that sense, Arthur was in better shape than the other traders we have discussed were. When Arthur came to a better understanding of what was important to him, he realized that he already had most of it. He had a strong and loving family, a successful business in which he could take pride and a place in his community in which he contributed. What he had been missing was a spiritual life. Once Arthur found that, he was able to get back to his trading, much to his wife's relief. In fact, he found that he was trading better than he had ever done before.

Looking for Signs

Before traders reach this mid-point in their lives, the first step they need to take is to start looking for the signs that things are changing and pay attention when they do. Our brains are programmed to detect the subtlest changes in our environment for our survival. We ignore them at our peril.

The second way to fend off a midlife trading crisis is to take excellent care of your physical and emotional selves, and of your most important relationships. If you are spending less time with your spouses, with your children, with your parents and your closest friends, you take the risk of waking up one day to find that they are gone forever and you have lost the chance to show them that you cared.

The third step is to take the time to figure out what is important to you. What are your goals? What kind of a life do you want to lead? What do you want your legacy to be when you leave the planet? What are the most meaningful things in your life? It is important to write these things down because they reinforce themselves in your mind when you put them on paper.

The fourth step is to handle your emotional and spiritual needs before they handle you. Far too many traders believe that all of their deepest needs will be taken care of if they ignore them and simply make enough money to buy their way out of emotional and spiritual pain. Eventually, however, the piper comes for his pay.

Conclusion

The best way to handle a midlife trading crisis is to not have one at all, and the best way to do that is to be prepared. If we take the time to figure out what a meaningful existence is for us, we will not be trapped in the day to day details of life, only to wake up and find that time has passed us by. The good news is that once we set our priorities, the passage of time will bring continued rewards, in our trading and in our personal lives.

SECTION 4
Strategies for Improving your Trading

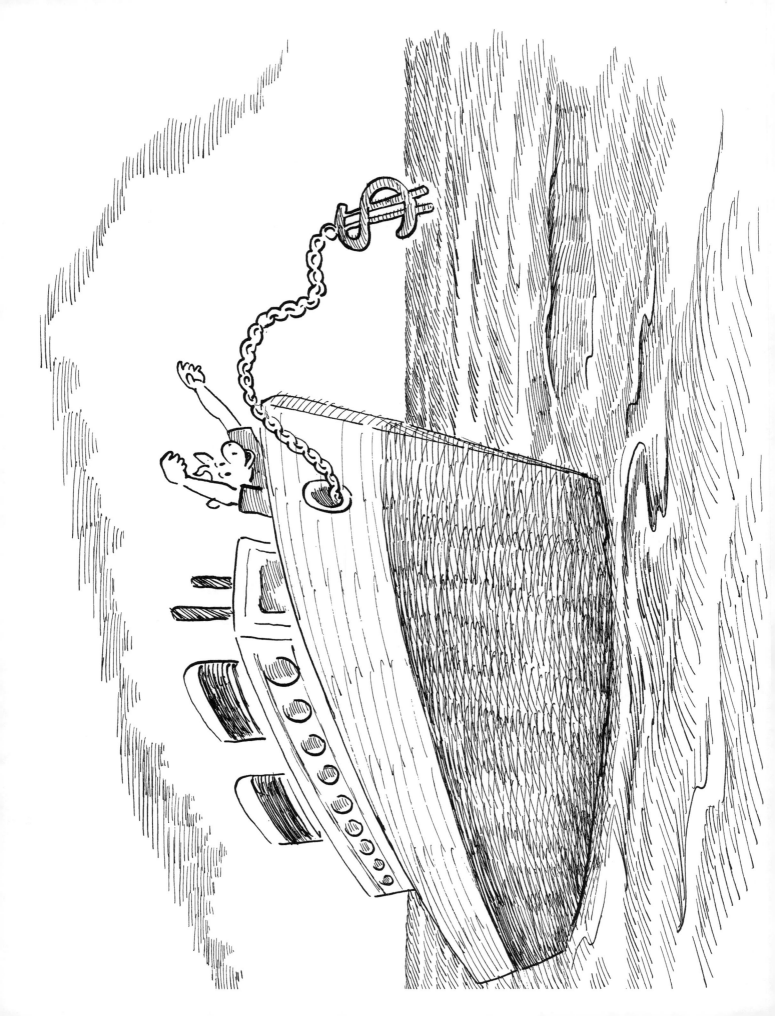

Chapter 15

_____

CREATING BETTER ANCHORS

Why do you trade the way you do and get the results that you get? To answer that question, you would likely discuss the logical reasons that you make decisions. You would describe the signals from your trading methodology, your years of training in the markets, the gut feelings that you get, and the hard-won disciplines that you have developed. However, these rational and conscious decisions and actions very often fail to answer this all-important question. Instead of heeding conscious commands, much of what we do is driven by unconscious motivations, associations, and signals of which we are completely unaware.

In the past, the popular press has constantly printed articles about how we as humans only use a small fraction of our brain's capacity. The implication was that the rest of the brain that appeared to be unused was available for us to employ if we could only figure out what to do with it. By learning to harness this unused capacity, what geniuses we could become and how successful we could truly be!

Making Associations

However, in recent years, scientists have found that most of that "unused capacity" is actually designated for use as associative faculties. So, in fact, we really are using this unused brain capacity; we are using it in associating one thing with another. When we see one thing, it reminds us of something else. This happens all day long, day in and day out. We associate everything that comes into the field of our five senses with all of the things that we have stored away in our associative storage files.

This ability to associate one thing with another is our way of saving time by figuring out immediately what something is or is like, so we know how to relate to it. In addition, it is a built-in survival mechanism. When we find something that reminds us of nothing else, it is a great revelation and cause for excitement or alarm. If we know how to categorize something immediately, we know instantly whether to fight or run.

For example, when we see a burner on the stove that looks red, we might associate it with our mother's voice yelling to us as children, "Stay away from the burner! You'll get burned!!" And maybe, we also associate it with that terrible, painful burn we got when we failed to heed her, and the fact that we spent the summer recuperating instead of playing baseball with our friends.

Creating Anchors

Now, whenever we see a red burner, we have two instantaneous reactions. The first is to pull away from the hot burner. The second is to feel fear and pain. These two reactions, one physical and the other emotional, are associations that we make by reaching into those large memory banks in our brains once thought to be "mental dustbins." These associations are experienced so rapidly and automatically that we may not even be aware of them except that we may feel vaguely uncomfortable.

That red burner now has meaning for us. It has become an anchor. Every time we see it, we anchor ourselves to a set of reactions and associations. We do not question the anchor or its associations unless things keep going wrong for us. For example, if the association we made with that red burner was not pain and fear but pleasure, we would be a card-carrying member of the burn unit at the local hospital. How could that happen? Suppose that instead of feeling upset that you lost the summer to a painful recovery, you were forced to miss school. Instead, you stayed home, watched television, ate ice cream, and were waited on hand and foot by your mother, fussed over by everyone and made to feel like a hero. You might feel differently about red-hot burners then.

Many anchors do not have such a traumatic association. Some anchors have very positive associations and produce very positive actions and feelings in us. For example, a positive anchor could be that every time you sit down in your special desk chair and turn on your reading light, you are overcome with a peaceful sense that everything in your life is under control. At that moment, you are able to tackle any problem that comes your way in a relaxed, mature, and effective way. This type of anchor is welcome because it supports your life.

Trading and Anchors

When we understand which anchors we have created in our trading, we will understand why we act and react the way we do and get the results that we do. We can begin to see why we respond to certain signals in a particular way. If those anchors are positive ones, we will move forward. But, if they bring fear, doubt, powerlessness, or greed, we will progress in a much different direction.

Neuro-Linguistic Programming (NLP) is one of the best tools available to study anchors and the role that they play in our lives. As an NLP-trained coach, when a trader comes to me for help, one of the first things that I do is to figure out what his anchors are, both negative and positive.

One of my recent clients named Dan had developed a costly anchor. Dan lost a lot of money by taking a particular type of signal. The fear and pain he experienced during and after these trades had made an indelible impression upon him. As a result, Dan was unable to trade this particular signal. Each time he saw this signal, he reacted as though it were a red-hot burner. Dan's anchor was so powerful that he could not, even if he knew how to, undo this association by himself. This resulted in large losses that only deepened the anchor.

Once we were able to identify the problem, Dan and I were able to undo the negative association with this signal so that he could associate it with potential earnings and no longer react from fear. The result was that Dan was once again making profits in his trading.

At the same time that you want to identify those anchors that are holding you back, you also want to identify those that are moving you forward. Last year, I worked with a highly successful trader who was making a great deal of money. What he wanted was to reach the next level of success. The way to do that was to find what had made him successful to date. We identified which anchors produced successful associations and results and focused on using them. The result was that he significantly increased his profits in one year.

Recognizing Anchors

The first step to creating the right anchors for your trading is to identify the ones that you have now. The following exercise will help you to do this. This exercise will require you to stop and notice what is happening every time you take a trade. Pay attention to the specific steps you take and how you feel at each step. If the process is smooth and easy, with no hesitation, and you are consistent about when you take your entries, just keep doing what you are doing. However, if, like too many traders, your entry becomes a tug of war between you and fear or between you and uncertainty, you must note everything that you are doing at that moment so you can make some other choices.

Before we discuss how to recognize what you are doing in making better or different choices, we need to lay a foundation of what is necessary to get to this step. First, you must have a system or methodology that you believe will bring good results if you follow it. If this is not true, return to square one and redo your business plan or create a business plan, if you do not have one. Make certain that you have some sort of testing methodology to create a sense of confidence that you will make money. That being said, I will assume that if you are reading on, it is because the only thing that is keeping you from success are old, negative anchors that you have created as a result of losses or some other psychological issues.

This article is not about handling all psychological issues. It is about changing or recreating anchors that you have established which have trapped you in the same old patterns.

Exercise

1. Recognize what you are physically doing before taking a trade and during a trade. For example, are you sitting down, standing up, are you ten inches from the screen, on the phone, or picking up the phone? What are you doing?

2. What is your strategy for taking the trade? Do you see a signal, recognize that it is familiar, feel good about it, and take the trade? Hear a voice in your head that is negative, then enter too late? Or, not take the trade at all? Strategies are not always easily recognized by the person who is executing them. However, if you pay close attention and ask yourself the following questions, you should be able to come up with, at least, the location of the stumbling block: What do I do next? What do I think next? What do I feel next?

3. Very often, it is the words that you say to yourself and the result of the negative pictures that you get in your head that creates the anchors. Therefore, you need to pay attention to what you say to yourself, the pictures those sounds create and the action that follows.

Creating a Positive Anchor

Once you have identified your negative anchors, the next step is to change the anchor by changing the sense memory that creates the anchor.

Here is an example of one trader describing what happens when he sets a negative anchor:

- Usually the voice comes at the end of the day, when I have had a bad run or when I am tired.
- I am looking at the chart and my computer identifies an opportunity.
- I am sitting down, leaning forward.
- The voice in my head is deliberate, loud, and fast. It is my father's voice.
- The voice is saying, "Suppose I am wrong - Suppose I lose."
- An unresourceful state of fear is located in my gut.

Using this description, here is an example of a way to change the negative anchor:

- Make a rule that you will not trade unless you are in a Peak Performance State.
- Mentally rehearse a particular scenario when this anchor would not allow for winning action.
- Remember when you were in a Peak Performance State and notice where you are now re-creating the feeling. Say one word to describe the feeling, for example, "Confident."
- In your mind's eye see yourself stand up or go into another position or put on a hat when your computer identifies an opportunity.

- When you begin to hear the voice, make it sound like Mickey Mouse - then say "Cancel, Cancel."
- Change the words and voice to say, "I make money when I follow my rules."
- Re-ignite your Peak Performance State by saying, "Confident."
- See yourself taking the trade successfully.
- Continue to mentally rehearse this several times until it becomes automatic.

Conclusion

Each trader unknowingly creates anchors in his trading. Some of these anchors are positive and others are negative. These anchors are powerful, unconscious guides to the trading actions a trader takes and the results that he gets. However, once a trader learns to identify the anchors that he has and the steps required to create new and better anchors, he has the ability to create and select better anchors for himself. These new anchors will tie the day-to-day stimuli around him to the very acts and feelings that empower him to be a highly successful trader.

Chapter 16

USING YOUR INTELLIGENCE

Do You Have the Intelligence to Become Extremely Wealthy?

Before you answer that question, you should consider whether you also have the right kind of intelligence to create an extraordinary life.

For years, the general public has accepted the mistaken belief that there is only one kind of intelligence. As children, we took the standard IQ tests that pigeonholed us into categories attempting to predict our individual ability to succeed in life. Unfortunately, most people bought into this limited thinking about intelligence and did not attempt to go beyond what they were told they could achieve.

However, anecdotal evidence and long-term studies have appeared indicating that the smartest kid in the class may not have ended up as the richest person of the group or with the most satisfying life. People have begun to question the value of these IQ tests since they are not predictive of success, even in the academic environment. It has become clear that other forms of intelligence are vital to people's success.

The Different "Types" of Intelligence

1. Linear Intelligence
This is the form of intelligence measured by IQ tests. It is the logical, linear thought that is adept at using numbers and words in the step-by-step process to solve problems. Linear thought depends upon information that is given or stored to reach logical conclusions. This intelligence is one of the types of intelligence vital to people who need to understand material from books and translate the information into knowledge useful in their profession. Certain professionals, such as accountants, lawyers and doctors, require this type of intelligence to pass the qualifying exams to enter these professions and master the knowledge and skills required to practice their professions.

2. Street Savvy

We all know someone who has more street sense than anyone else. This kind of savvy or intelligence is vital to survival in risky situations. Yet, highly "intelligent" individuals are often at a loss to quickly solve the problems of survival on the streets of their real world. The sources of information used in street savvy are not obvious, nor are the conclusions logical or arrived at in a step-by-step process. This intelligence is vital to those careers that require second-to-second decisions based on a synergistic understanding and awareness of all of the cues that are available to the individual at that moment. Often the stakes of a situation are high and time is in short supply. Fighter pilots, surgeons, trial attorneys, floor traders, negotiators, and police officers all need to react instantaneously. This intelligence often has a foundation of linear intelligence, but goes beyond learned logic to experienced flow.

3. Wisdom

This kind of intelligence is a deep knowing that is vital to people who go beyond the norm and become masters at their chosen field. It includes information that is available through Universal Consciousness. You will find wisdom in seers, telepaths, as well as inventors, ministers, rabbis, artists, philosophers, and grandparents. Connecting to the collective wisdom beyond your own develops this type of intelligence.

4. Emotional Intelligence

Individuals who do not know how to detect social cues, develop relationships, or handle their emotional state lack Emotional Intelligence. The individuals who have Emotional Intelligence are good at running service-oriented businesses, being entrepreneurs and having management positions. This type of intelligence is absolutely vital to the success of anyone who requires a high level of self-discipline to be successful. Emotional intelligence provides the ability for an individual to manage his emotional and social life so he or she can set and attain goals. In addition, it enables one to get support from the significant people who are the building blocks to each new level of success.

5. Mechanical/Spatial Intelligence

Have you ever had a great mechanic work on your car? I mean someone who was literally a genius with machines. This type of intelligence allows individuals to understand how things work and/or to see things in spatial terms, but not necessarily in numerical or intellectual terms. Great athletes like Michael Jordan fit into this category. It is not just training and physical prowess that allowed him to judge the distances in the air for those jumps and shots that took our breath away. This type of intelligence is vital in learning to use computers to their full potential. It is also a resource for people who must travel in their work because travel to new places can be disorienting and time-consuming if you lack spatial intelligence.

6. Creative/Artistic Intelligence

Artists, musicians, and all other creative people use their sense of detail to combine, enhance, and restructure information. Creative people have the ability to go beyond a linear and structured view of the world. This form of intelligence enables them to see and discover opportunities in places that elude others. It is necessary to have creative ability as well as a logical ability to be able to master any profession.

Which Form of Intelligence Does a Highly Successful Person Have?

To become a true master of an endeavor requires more than any single type of intelligence. Most people rely on just one or two types of intelligence, but to rise above the crowd requires several types of intelligence to be combined, if not a bit of all of them. Developing any new aspect of intelligence will increase your ability to earn greater profits and enjoy a better life. Adding a new dimension to your intelligence will increase your self-confidence and provide more insight for making the best choices.

Developing and Expanding your Intelligence

Now that you are aware of the various forms of intelligence, you may be saying to yourself, "Great, but what can I do about it? I have a fixed IQ. My EQ is so low that puppies avoid me. I have no creative intelligence. My street smarts couldn't help me out of a brawl with five-year olds. I have no mechanical/spatial sense, and wisdom has thus far escaped me."

The question is, of course, "Is there anything that can be done to develop or expand your various forms of intelligence?" The answer is a qualified "Yes." If you are sufficiently committed to the process, there are many strategies to expand your intelligence. This does not imply that you will suddenly become a mechanical genius or set the social world on end, but I have helped and watched others develop an intelligence that was once totally lacking in their day-to-day activities. What these remarkable transformations required, in each case, was a commitment to the goal and the willingness to do things that were difficult.

Alternate forms of intelligence are often like weak muscles that have never been used because they required a great deal of effort to produce results. For many people, the effort has never seemed worthwhile because, lacking great natural talent in this area, the process of developing this new skill meant a degree of discomfort, failure, slow progress, and poor feedback. Often, these alternate forms of intelligence are present but dormant. What appears to be the creation of this new intelligence is merely the nurturing of a talent that was hidden. Even if the latent talent is modest, often its potential can be enhanced or maximized.

Step One
Identify the area of intelligence that you feel is lacking. Make an assessment of your present level of competence.

Step Two

You must come to this process with the strongly held belief that you DO have some latent talent in this area and that, if you give the process a real effort, you will begin to see progress. Visualize yourself more creative, more socially skilled, more wise, savvy, and mechanically/spatially aware.

Step Three

Become conscious of how you perform in the area without becoming judgmental. This is a very important step because it allows you to observe and eventually correct shortcomings without holding you back with negative feelings and self-talk.

Step Four

Find someone who epitomizes the intelligence you would like to improve and study him or her. Discover how this person thinks by listening to their beliefs, values, decisions, and attitudes. Ask them what lessons they have learned along the way.

Step Five

Find a tutor, teacher, or mentor who can give you personalized guidance and feedback.

Working on Your Own to Improve Your Intelligence

Intellectual

Read or listen to non-fiction, how-to books with a predetermined notion of what you want to get out of the book. Highlight all salient material and learn the material as if you had to teach it to someone else. Enroll in courses in history, philosophy, literature or science and make certain that there is no grade attached to the course so that you can focus on learning. Approach the subject with enthusiasm and confidence.

Street Savvy

Street savvy depends upon information, experience, strategy, and interaction. Learn the details of every part of the task or job. For example: If you are a salesman, be sure to use the product you are selling as well as the competition's product. If you are a corporate leader, go down to the mailroom and learn the jobs that keep your company functioning. Then, go over to the kitchen and learn the cook's job. You are not there just to learn the job, but how to interact with the people who are performing its tasks. Street savvy comes from being able to play the hand you are dealt regardless of the players or the action. One of the best ways to develop street savvy is to learn how to play poker to win.

Wisdom

Learn to meditate. Isolate yourself for extended periods of time without outside stimulation. Be willing to reach inside yourself for answers and learn to trust the answers that come without any sense of fear attached.

Emotional

Most people cannot develop their emotional intelligence in a vacuum. You need to find experiences that will provide constructive, supportive feedback. For example, take a class in sales, join Toastmasters, your local theater group, a support group, or a group therapy class. Take a parenting class or work as a volunteer with children or adults.

Mechanical/spatial

Unravel spatial puzzles or take a small machine apart and put it back together. Take a course in car repair or tackle some home repairs that you normally reserve for a paid handyman. Spend time studying maps and take the navigator's seat on trips.

Creative

Take an art class, music lessons, or write a story and then have someone correct it. Keep reworking it until it makes sense. Go to art museums or listen to classical music.

Conclusion

Just as you cannot gain skills in any part of your life without practice and confidence, you cannot expand an undeveloped part of your intelligence without a commitment of time and energy. As you make progress, reward yourself. Your brain will respond to this feedback by giving you more reasons to be rewarded. Often, we fail to develop our intelligence in certain areas because we have special learning needs, like a left-handed child who is forced to write with his right hand. So, we fail to do well and then refuse to try later on. With these steps, you will make progress in maximizing your full intelligence and the results will soon begin to show up in the bottom line of having a good life. And yes, you will also develop the ability to become wealthier.

Chapter 17
_____

PAYING THE PRICE FOR SUCCESS

Every individual comes into life with a set of resources that add to or detract from his energy and ability to live a successful life. As a person develops into adulthood, he can either add to or delete from his personal collection of resources.

Ed was born with exceptional aptitude, creative skills, and good health. Adding to his natural resources, he was raised in a loving, supportive family that inspired him to do whatever he wanted to do and to become the best person he could be. When Ed decided to become a trader, it came easily to him. It appeared that the price he had to pay for his success was small because the deck was stacked in his favor, and he worked to keep it that way. Life required very little sacrifice from Ed and the challenges that he had were enjoyable parts of his journey.

Ed is the rare exception. Most traders have a substantial price to pay for their success in trading. The price exacted is largely determined by the type of trader someone wants to be and the kind of returns they expect to have. For instance, if a trader wants to trade mutual funds part-time on a long-term basis, he will need a much different set of resources than a full-time futures trader who trades 5-minute charts on-line.

Are You Willing to Pay the Price to be a Professional Trader?

What is the Price?

The cost of successful trading can be calculated by adding up the costs in terms of:

1. **Physical Health**
   To be an effective trader over the long haul requires "a high frequency of energy" that is supported by good physical health. If you are not physically healthy, you will not have the emotional and mental strength necessary to make quick and effective choices. Operating from a low frequency of energy, a trader will succumb to fear and

insecurities. A habitual pattern of negative thinking will lead to negative behaviors that become familiar to your neurological system and, therefore, more deeply imbedded in it.

Think of yourself as an athlete in training who needs to maintain a healthy diet, and an adequate amount of exercise and relaxation. When your trading results are not reflecting what your system is capable of giving you, improve your health and you will more than likely improve your trading results.

2. Mental Health

The same significance should be placed on mental health as physical limitations. As a person lives his life, he accumulates negative issues that were not resolved at the time they were experienced. As an adult, the tendency is to brush away these issues by recognizing them and understanding that they once existed. Understanding the problem will not heal or resolve the issue. These issues will show up as sabotaged performance in trading. This is especially true when you are operating at a "low frequency of energy."

You will have to handle emotional issues with a professional if you want to get the most out of your ability as a trader. Those who choose to handle psychological issues sooner rather than later end up ahead of the game.

3. Environmental Support

When a trader does not feel that he was supported in the things he wanted to do as a child, it usually translates to internal conflict as an adult. A part of him will support his trading activities because that is what he wants to do, but his parents' voices, which are also a part of him, will usually win the conflict. He will find it difficult to enter a trade.

As an adult, if a trader's family is not supportive, he will feel guilty when he does not make money and resentment when he does or he will feel ambivalent towards his family. None of these feelings is conducive to a good trading state of mind.

If you believe that you will succeed and have made good choices in becoming a trader, you will be more likely to get the support of significant people around you. The confidence you exude will make them feel more confident in you. Of course, nothing builds confidence like evidence of success. The problem usually starts, however, while you are on your way to building that evidence. It is important to make sure that you educate the people in your life to realize that trading is a viable way to earn a living. Show them your business plan and discuss the reasons that you believe you can make a success in this business by modeling those who are successful.

4. Trained in Technical and Creative Skills

To be a well-rounded trader, the left technical side of the brain and the right creative side of the brain need to be stimulated. Technical studies such as math and science develop a trader's understanding for the logical part of trading. Studies such as music, art, and drama develop the creative part of a trader's understanding. The balance between the logical and creative sides of the brain develops intuition, which is the seed of artistry and mastery in a trader.

One of the ways to develop the logical side of the brain is to play games requiring math skills. The creative side of the brain can be exercised by creating stories in your mind and on paper, in sensorial detail.

5. Education in the Markets

Trading is like any other profession it must be studied. Would a doctor or lawyer read one book and consider himself trained? The more understanding a trader has about all aspects of the market, the more he will know how to prepare for contingencies. If he plans for contingencies, he will not have as many lessons as most traders who fail their way to becoming a trader.

Start reading books on the markets in general. Then, read books that are specific to the area of interest you have in trading. Keep building your library with books, tapes, courses, and conferences.

6. Self-Discipline

All endeavors requiring sacrifice, time commitment, and following rules, are training for the discipline necessary to become a trader. If a trader cannot follow his system or methodology, it is either because he does not believe in his system, he has never exercised discipline and does not know how, or there is some psychological block.

A simple way to develop discipline is to make a weekly, then daily plan. Follow the plan while adding more detail to the plan each week.

7. Passion – Motivation – Commitment

A trader needs motivation and commitment to persist in overcoming the challenges to becoming a successful trader over the long haul. This commitment and motivation is stimulated by passion.

Think in detail about something that you want to accomplish and see a positive end result. Notice how passion builds when you become emotionally charged. Passionate living is developed from passionate dreaming. Taking the extra steps to make an event or an experience more enriching creates the passion needed to motivate you to the top of any profession.

8. Trading Capital

The fact is that you cannot be a trader if you do not have enough money with which to trade. If you trade with too little money, you will most likely lose it all. Few traders have the psychology necessary to trade part-time with a small bankroll, slowly building it until they can trade full time.

Develop a financial report of resources that you have and compare it to resources that you will need to become a trader. Consider your living and business expenses in addition to the risk capital for trading. Then, make a financial goal outlining when you will be able to start trading. In the meantime, develop your trading plan and keep studying the markets, so that when the money is there to begin, you will have the skills necessary for successful trading.

9. Time

Too many traders attempt two professions at one time, which creates a great deal of stress. Ideally, a trader should develop and begin to trade a system in a stress-free state of mind. If a trader constantly puts himself under time pressure, he will most likely develop negative issues such as failed relationships and failed health, which will lead to the inability to follow trading rules.

Plan your time to include a balanced life. Get the cooperation from the significant people in your life supporting your plan for trading and allowing the time necessary to develop yourself as a trader.

If Ed had made the lifestyle choices of drinking alcohol excessively and taking drugs while living in a polluted environment, he would have given away his health resource. Giving up health could have led to the loss of other positive resources that he had for being a balanced trader. If, on the other hand, Ed had made healthy choices, went on to get a Masters' Degree in Finance, learned to play jazz saxophone, and created his own supportive family as an adult, he would have added to the resources that he was given as a child. His positive choices would have made his path to becoming a trader more easy to follow.

Another Way of Looking at It

Let's say that in your particular life situation, you need 100 points of energy to maintain the balance necessary for a positive attitude and good choices in life. If your energy drops below 100 points, you fall into a pit of negativity and sabotage. This can occur from anything that rattles you such as bad news or even as a result of your low energy portion of the day. To keep from falling into the pit, it would be necessary for you to maintain an average of 120 points of energy, giving you a range of fluctuation in the positive zone. If you add position trading to your mix of activities, it would be necessary for you to maintain 150 points of energy because the swings of emotional volatility will probably be greater. To be an electronic day-trader working one-minute charts, you might have to maintain an energy level of 200 points to keep from going into the pit.

Observe what it takes for you to maintain focus and stability to know if you are making enough positive choices to keep yourself out of the pit. Maybe you need to add another hour of sleep or a protein bar as a snack in the afternoon. It is important to note that it becomes harder to pull yourself out of the pit after several times because the reserve to draw on becomes depleted.

114

The Monkey Wrench

The combination of resources that Joe had as a floor trader made him a great deal of money. Yet, his lifestyle choices were certainly not the model for a long-term, successful trading career. He lived on junk food, drank heavily, and was a party animal almost every night. Despite his lifestyle choices, he maintained a five hundred thousand-dollar per year income for seven years.

Joe's best friend died in a plane crash, which put him into a deep state of depression. Far down in the pit, Joe had no reserves to get out because he had been drawing heavily on his personal energy account for so long. When Joe got back into trading, he lost his rhythm and his confidence. His bad habits intensified as he went deeper and deeper into the pit with no rescue line that could reach far enough to save him.

Conclusion

Each trader has a price to pay for success. Some pay the price over the course of their lives, while others have to make a consolidated payment over a very brief period of time. In either case, the more resources a trader has at his disposal, the less likely it is that he will sabotage his trading career. By maintaining good choices, it is less likely that a trader will fall into a pit of sabotage, and if he does, he will have the resources that provide the ability to bounce back out.

Chapter 18

FULL TIME TRADING

"I Work Eight Hours, I Sleep Eight Hours, And I Have Eight Hours Of Fun."

Trading full time can translate to anything from grueling sixteen-hour workdays to one hour per day or any combination of time in between. It is important to discover what time frame is right for you in order to get the most benefit out of your trading results while maintaining a good and happy life. Too many traders get trapped into thinking that they should put a certain amount of time into their trading day and the amount of time that they choose can be either too much or too little for getting the best results.

He works Hard for the Money

Being a consistently profitable trader takes just as much time and energy as any profession where rewards can be exceptional. The problem for many traders is that the pattern of long hours becomes an addictive behavior that is difficult to overcome. Traders begin to think that if they do not keep up with long hours, their trading results will suffer. It is highly advisable for traders to put a considerable amount of time into study while they are in the process of becoming a trader. But, if a trader continuously pressures himself for too long, the imbalance in his life will have an adverse effect on his trading results. For a trader to maintain a consistent top performance level, he must be physically, emotionally, spiritually and socially in balance. In short, this means that he must also have a life beyond trading.

It Ain't Necessarily So

The old work ethic would have you believe that in order to earn a living from your work, you must work at least eight hours per day. By observing the patterns of clients, I have found that many of them would earn considerably more money if they did not put as many hours into their trading.

Sometimes it Takes a Coach…

1. **To Point it Out to Them**
   When I restate to a client what he has verbalized to me about the activities of his trading day, he becomes aware of the obvious solution, which is to use his time more effectively. For example, Ron traded on the floor of the exchange for years. He has been diligent to be there at the opening and closing of almost every day for the last 10 years. He has consistently made money, but working in the pits has taken its toll on his body to the point that trading has stopped being fun.

   He said to me, "Yeah, sometimes I think it's just a waste of my time to come in the afternoons. I lose a lot of the money that I make in the mornings because I've never been good with handling volatility when I'm tired." I asked him, "What do you imagine your results would be if you hadn't traded in the afternoons for the last five years?" He said, "Hell, I'd be ahead by twice the amount, or more."

   Now, Ron is trading only in the mornings, enjoying the rest of the day at the gym and feeding the ducks by the lake. He is also earning considerably more money than he was and is enjoying trading once again.

2. **To Recognize the Patterns Themselves**
   The best way to improve your system or methodology is to be consistent in following your trading rules over a period of time. Patterns will emerge showing when and where you earn the most profits. Sometimes, a trader is too close to notice it himself. In Tom's case, he simply did not want to notice the obvious.

   Tom was trading two time frames. Trading the long-term time frame was supporting the short-term trading and his life style. After I held a mirror up to Tom so that he would admit to his day trading gambling addiction, he decided to choose computer war games as a substitute for his compulsions. Now, he is earning a full-time salary working one hour per day on his long-term position trading.

3. **To Get Permission from Someone to Work Less**
   Traders get models of what is an appropriate amount of working time from their parents, their teachers, their peers, and other traders. Most of them don't get to experience the many good traders who work a shorter day and earn good profits doing so. They are more likely to believe someone like me, a Trader's Coach, because of the vast experience I have had working with many traders than people in their family who tell them the same thing. For example:

   When Marty first started trading, he made mistakes that cost him a great deal of money. Since his mistakes, he felt that he had to rethink his trading decisions over and over before he made a final decision. I asked him how many times did he have to look at a chart before he recognized an opportunity. "Only once," was his response. Marty finally understood that he did not have to recheck himself and it was okay to

118

spend less time analyzing the markets. In fact, he is making more money now, feels less stressed, and has more time for his family and friends.

4. **To Plan to do Something that is Compelling with the Extra Time**
Watching a trading screen for some traders is more exciting than other activities in their lives. For people who love this intensity, trading is hard to walk away from unless there is something equally compelling to anticipate. For example:

Tim once had a wife, children, community activities, and hobbies to keep him balanced and happy. His wife who was his "activities director" passed away and his children went out on their own. Tim did not know how to do things on his own. He started spending more and more time behind the computer screen until it consumed all of his time. He missed his old life, but did not know how to get himself interested in other things beyond trading.

When I worked with him, I gave him weekly assignments of activities that he had to accomplish. At first, he was reluctant and told me that all of my suggestions were not as interesting as sitting and watching the screen. One week some old friends asked him to a party. Normally, he would have refused, but I insisted that he attend the party as his weekly assignment. At the party, he met a woman who was like his wife and had a very active social life. She took over as his "social director" and he is back to a balanced happy life working on trading six hours per day instead of sixteen and is earning just as much if not more money.

5. **To Convince the Significant People Around You that Working a Shorter Day Does not Mean that You have Become a Handy Man**
When one member of a family is working 10 to12 hours per day and making perhaps half as much money as the trader in the family, it sometimes becomes an issue that their spouse is not at least "putting in his time" for the hard stuff in the relationship. Many traders waste time at the screen because they do not want to become the errand boy or the Mr. Mom that would be expected of them if they did not sit behind the screen all day. Here is an example.

Linda was always complaining that her trader husband, Harry, failed to get chores done around the house. I suggested that Harry ask Linda for a list of the chores to be completed and agree that if the chores got done, he could do what he wanted with his time. Harry found people to handle most of the handyman stuff. As a result, he spent less time at the screen and easily handled the added expense with the increase in income working fewer stressed hours.

6. **To Prepare so that they do not Feel that they are Missing out on Something**
Every trader has a war story of the big trade that they missed when their attention was diverted from the screen. For this reason, traders glue themselves to the screen through countless hours waiting for the 'big one' to hit. Most of the best traders that I know do not look for killings, but consistently pull profits out of every day trading. These traders at the top pace themselves to have a life while enjoying the time that

they do spend trading. This strategy prevents the build up of tension that most traders develop by not allowing themselves time away from the screens. For example:

Yes, there was that time that Joe missed that big trade when his wife dragged him away on vacation. And yes, there was that time when he was sick that afternoon and missed another big trade. He still talks about the big trades that got away. He was spending so much time watching the screen that he over-traded and missed opportunities that were smaller fortunes. I asked Joe to give up 50% of his trades and work a four-hour day for one month and check the results. While he reluctantly committed to my suggestions, he accomplished giving up 20% of his normal trades and worked a six-hour day. He made more money in that month than ever before. He was still uncomfortable, but the profits were strong evidence that he was not missing larger profits by gluing himself to the screen in his effort to catch the next 'big one.'

7. To Protect Themselves from Possible Losses that Could Occur

Albert was in the habit of watching his stops <u>very</u> closely. Often, he would lower his stop thinking that it would get hit and the market would immediately bounce back. It was not okay for him to be wrong and lose money on a position. He forced himself to watch the screen for most of his waking day and sometimes through the night. Albert was exhausted and a nervous wreck. I pointed out the obvious when he told me his problem. In order for him to trust himself, he was going to have to commit to his stops and feel that he could walk away from the screen. I suggested that he go back to his trading plan. He needed to work on contingencies for his rules and backtest all of the positions that he had taken to see what the results would have been if he had kept to his original stops. What he found was that he would have made more money if he had consistently stayed with his original stops. We worked on his issues of the fear of being wrong. We also worked on mentally rehearsing feeling comfortable trading his rules and staying with his initial stop loss. Now, he is able to leave the screen with confidence that his rules for stop placement are the best for his method. Albert works a four-hour day and is well rested for making better choices.

8. To Say It's Time to Call it a Day

Here are some questions for you to coach yourself. They will help you recognize if you are using the right amount of time to produce the best results.

- Why do you work the hours that you work?
- What would happen if you worked fewer hours?
- When do you make most of your money?
- How much of your day do you waste?
- What part of the day do you make most of your money?
- What part of the day do you make the least amount of money?
- Who expects you to put in a certain amount of hours to be considered full time?
- Would you make more money if you worked less or more hours?

Conclusion

Successful trading initially demands many hours of studying and planning. One of the difficulties and/or benefits of being a professional trader is that the traditional eight hour work day is not necessarily the rule for getting the most in monetary reward. While some traders need those extra hours to produce great profits in the markets, I have found that many traders who lessen the hours that they spend in the markets produce better results.

Chapter 19

TELLING YOUR FUTURE

The best way to make money in the markets is by having the ability to predict the future. While you continuously receive the message that "the past doesn't equal the future," there are some indicators, which when monitored can give you an advantage over the future.

The Past that Influences the Future

No single source of information is as helpful in predicting how you will fare in the markets as the backtesting of your trading methodology. Backtesting provides the history of the markets while demonstrating how your particular methodology or system would have fared over a period of time. Backtesting a system also conditions your responses to the flow of the markets. This practice prepares your neurology to be "at one with the markets." In other words, as you backtest, you develop an anchor to the flow of the markets giving you a discretionary, intuitive indicator that is reliable. When you trade with an intuitive indicator, your trading goes beyond science and mathematics and becomes an art.

Fundamental analysis and technical analysis are the building blocks that prepare you for all conditions in the markets. Technique alone can make you a steady, good trader, but to become a top trader requires that your creative side merge with your logical side. To understand this concept, let's go outside of the world of trading to find some parallels for what it takes to become great:

1. A surgeon who has read all the books and received top scores in his classes is not necessarily the best doctor. The doctor who has a feel for what is happening in the flow of the human body is more likely to be able to go beyond the books when something comes up in surgery that would have the "book learning doctors" stumped.

2. A great trial lawyer must choose the right words and actions to influence the judge and

each member of a jury to convince them to accept his side of an argument. This effort requires second by second choices that cannot always come from a textbook.

3. A great jazz musician goes beyond one note at a time. The connection with the music, other musicians, the audience and with himself has to be a synergistic balance that flows beyond technique.

In this year's Final Four when the Duke and Maryland basketball teams were playing, Duke was down by twenty-two points in the first half. At half time, Coach K told his team to forget the deficit and go out and play from instinct. That bit of advice helped the Blue Devils to come back and win that game giving them the opportunity to go on to win another NCAA basketball championship.

Nurturing the Vehicle that Feeds Us

Just like great thoroughbred horses need to be fed the best grain, exercised and kept in a positive environment, a trader needs the same nurturing. If anything can have an influence on future conditions of performance, it would be how you take care of your choice-making vehicle. That vehicle is your mind, body and spirit. Some of the best traders have to be re-reminded about the basics of taking constant care of themselves. Too often, when you are making money, you are too busy maintaining momentum to properly care for yourself. Conversely, when you are not making money you are too busy trying to catch up.

The Future

If looking at the past can help you determine your fortune, can looking at the future be even more on target? One strategy for predicting the future is to find prognostic indicators that have a track record, i.e., when the wooly worms are exceptionally wooly, the winters are cold; when the stock market takes a crash, the economy follows; when our favorite market prophet says the market is going up, it does. Have you noticed that the way we evaluate good predictors of the future is to, once again, rely on the past? If their predictions in the past were highly accurate, their likelihood of being accurate next time is probably good.

The problem is that all predictive sources are fallible. Hanging your star on just one of them can lead to catastrophe. Still, we have learned to trust these sources to be as accurate as any predictive source can be.

The Psychology of the Past

Another way to tell your fortune by looking into the past is to look at your own psychological history. Recently, a trader told me that he had spent the weekend writing out his own history, including all of the events in his life, all of the players in his life, and all of his emotional history. He added the last part because he wanted to know who he was and how he had reacted to what had happened to him.

"I am planning my future," he said, "and these are rocky times that we are going through. This time I want to be in charge of my life. The only way I can do that is to understand who I am." This man is a very unusual person to begin with but his point is a good one. If you are going to predict your own future, you must know your past, and your psychological history is a major factor in that past.

Part of your psychological history could include your emotional patterns. For example: how have your emotional states paralleled the events in your life and how have they affected them? Have you ever been subject to depression, fits of anger, jealousy, sadness, lack of passion, resentment or bitterness? On the other hand, have you enjoyed long periods of emotional stability, happiness, excitement about life, contentment and hopefulness? What is the historical progression of your emotional life? For example, you may have started out as a spontaneous, optimistic and happy young child but turned into an angry and rebellious teen, then a jaded and pessimistic young adult who was subject to depression. Now, as a forty year old, you have achieved a level of maturity and balance. You are no longer pessimistic, but you have never felt a great deal of passion or joy since childhood. With a profile like this one, you would want to find out what turned the tide for that happy youngster? What caused that emotional transformation? And what has been the result of that pessimistic emotional state on various conditions?

Predicting Your Own Future

As methodical as we are in predicting the future of the markets, most traders do not give a second thought to predicting their own futures. And yet, the future is where their fortunes lie. If we had a handle on our own futures, we could make better plans, feel a great deal more peace, and achieve more success while reaching our goals.

What would happen if we took the strategies that we have developed for the markets and applied them to our futures and our fortunes?

1. **Strategy One**
    What have you done in similar markets and economic conditions? What are the results of your backtesting? What were your trading patterns, your profit histories, your ways of responding to various influences and conditions, and what were the results obtained from your methodologies? Which responses were the most fruitful? Assuming that you continued to behave the same way in the future, could the results be assumed to be the same as well? If that is the case, how do you feel about it? Does the picture that it generates make you happy? Does it take you where you want to go?

2. **Strategy Two**
    Based upon their track records, which predictors can give you accurate information about the future? For example, if you read articles in journals, books, or newsletters by specific individuals whose market predictions have been accurate in the past, are you reading them more closely now? What are they predicting and advising? Are

you following their advice? What can you expect to happen if they are right? What can you expect to happen if you apply the predictors that you have learned to trust to your trading? What will it say about your future? Is that what you want in your future?

3. Strategy Three

Your psychological history would show how you reacted emotionally during those times when the market was bearish, when it was flat, and when it was so unpredictable that you were constantly whipsawed and could not make profits. In other words, how did you react in the past when you were faced with losses and bad market conditions? Depending upon what you think is going to happen in the future, you can determine how you are probably going to feel and react. And, most importantly, you can determine the process that you used to survive and thrive.

When You do Not Like Your Future

At some point, you will have created a picture of your future. Suppose that you do not like what you foresee? Sometimes, telling your own trading future can be a very scary experience, but it can also provide you with a wake-up call that could change the entire picture for you. As they say in the sci-fi movies, the future is in your hands. Since the future is still unwritten, it means that you have wiggle room for change and can develop new strategies. For example:

- You can take immediate steps to prepare for the future to position yourself to benefit from it.
- You can evaluate your strengths, weaknesses, and assets to see what you have to work with.
- You can develop strategies to make allowances for your weaknesses. In the past, if you have panicked when the market hit a rocky road, do not allow the thinking that led up to the panic. Take immediate action to move in a positive direction.
- When you have a problem, ask for help immediately rather then waiting for your life to fall apart. The help can come from family, friends, associates, a book, a mentor, a seminar or a coach.

Psychological and Behavioral Patterns

You are programmed to think and behave in a pattern that is familiar. If this pattern is positive, productive and works on your behalf, then just allow your nature to unfold. If this pattern takes a hard course, then you must take the reins and consciously make different choices. Patterns are not easily changed without help, but it is possible with awareness and determination.

Conclusion

In the final analysis, your future is more likely to be predicted by the choices you make as you live your life. By analyzing your past, making better choice patterns, asking for help when necessary, and surrounding yourself with positive influences, you are more likely to create a future that is very fortunate.

SECTION 5
The Physical Side of Trading

Chapter 20

TRADERS AND SEROTONIN
PART 1

If the bottom line for trading is to make a profit, then the bottom line for making a profit is emotional well being. When a trader is feeling emotionally fit, he is armed with confidence, enthusiasm, optimism, a sense of self-worth, and the ability to focus on the action. In this peak emotional condition, he can make good trading decisions while maintaining self-discipline and following the rules of his trading methodology and money management strategy. Feeling good about himself and his life, he wants to take care of his health, his family, and his future.

In other words, this trader is prepared to win.

How many traders are trading with the level of emotional well being that arms them for success? Over the past decade, I have worked with many highly capable traders who are trying to win in the markets while dealing with depression, deep-seated pessimism, anxiety, hopelessness, and a lack of motivation or self-worth. These traders often have difficulty sleeping at night because their rest is interrupted by anxiety and restlessness. The next morning, they wake up with a sense of things not being exactly right in the world and a pervasive exhaustion. Handicapped with this excess baggage, they under-perform and lose when they should be winning, thus increasing their downward momentum. And these represent some of their good days!

The Science of Emotional Well Being

In recent years, the scientific and psychiatric communities have made extraordinary strides in understanding some of the biochemical causes of our emotional downturns, anxieties, and depressions. For top performers, one of the most exciting and far-reaching of these discoveries is the effect of the chemical messengers in our brain, called neurotransmitters, on our emotional and physical well being. Serotonin is generally considered to be the neurotransmitter that is most responsible for making us feel happy, calm, non-anxious, and rested. A deficiency in serotonin has been directly linked to

131

depression and its attendant symptoms as well as being directly and indirectly linked to the following:

1. the body's management of stress
2. the health of our circulatory and immune systems
3. our defense against cancer
4. our ability to sleep
5. the regulation of our endocrine system
6. obesity and uncontrollable appetite
7. anxiety and panic
8. bulimia
9. obsessive compulsive disorder
10. autism
11. social phobias
12. migraine headaches
13. rages
14. extreme violence
15. premenstrual syndrome
16. schizophrenia
17. attention deficit hyperactive disorder

While some of these far-reaching effects, like depression, are a direct result of low serotonin, some are caused indirectly by depression. For example, people who suffer from severe depression have an increased risk of dying after a heart attack or stroke and have poorer survival rates from cancer than those who are not depressed. Clearly, for the many traders who suffer from a serotonin problem, the implications of this research reach far beyond increasing their performance and can affect nearly every aspect of their sense of well being and future achievement.

In my research on this subject, I have come to suspect that as we get older and the more stress we are under from our careers, the more our diets are compromised, and the more we are exposed to the pollution that permeates our environment, the more likely we are to have reduced levels of serotonin. If you have not given this subject any thought, I would like to introduce you to the world of brain biochemistry. If you are currently taking anti-depressant drugs or other mood-altering substances, I would challenge you to look at this subject from the perspective of an educated consumer who is taking responsibility for his or her own course of treatment. For those of you who are fortunate enough to have perfectly working brain biochemistry, you may discover information that can help family members and associates whose moods and physical problems represent problems for you, as well.

What is Serotonin and Its Function?

In the human brain and nervous system, messages that travel from one nerve to another have one small problem: the nerves are not connected. Instead, there exists between them a space called a synapse. The messages that have traveled along the neuron on electrical impulse must now cross the synapse by means of a set of chemicals called neurotransmitters. Serotonin is considered the primary neurotransmitter that affects mood and emotions. Two other important neurotransmitters are norepinephrine (NR) and dopamine (DA), which also have an affect on mood and emotions.

The messenger serotonin is stored in little sacs at the end of each neuron. When an electrical impulse or message that needs to be transmitted stimulates the stored serotonin, it is released into the synapse and travels across and binds to the serotonin receptors at the end of the second neuron. Now that the message has been delivered, the serotonin needs to be neutralized, so it is either broken down or reabsorbed by the system. If serotonin were not removed from the synapse, it would build up and new messages would not get delivered. The enzyme that breaks down serotonin is called monoamine oxidase (MAO). When everything is working correctly, there is adequate serotonin to transmit the messages from one nerve to the other and there is the correct amount of MAO to break it down when the transmission is complete.

One of the by-products of serotonin is another brain chemical called melatonin, which regulates sleep and waking cycles. Again, when we are young and healthy and everything is working well, there is enough melatonin in our systems to help us fall asleep easily and get a good night's rest. But, without adequate serotonin, you will not produce enough melatonin, and may not get a good night's sleep.

As you can begin to see, there are very complicated chemical chain reactions taking place in our brain and nervous system that affect how we feel emotionally and physically. And the serotonin connection is just one tiny, but absolutely critical part of that chain.

Where Does Serotonin Come From?

The amount of serotonin in your brain is directly related to the amount of the amino acid, tryptophan, in your diet as well as your body's ability to utilize it. Amino acids are the essential building blocks of proteins that we must get from our diet. The best sources of the amino acid tryptophan come from meat, with turkey being one of the best sources. Fish, dairy products, soy protein, pumpkin and sesame seeds, lentils and bananas also contain significant amounts of tryptophan. Have you ever noticed how incredibly sleepy you feel after a Thanksgiving dinner? That need to take a nap was formerly attributed to having eaten a lot of food, especially food with a high fat and sugar content. However, you might have the same reaction if you only ate the turkey and the string beans, because turkey has such a significant amount of tryptophan in it.

If the serotonin problem could easily be corrected by ingesting more tryptophan, why not simply add it to our diets to increase the levels of serotonin or take tryptophan pills? Until 1988, there was a tremendously fast growing market for over-the-counter tryptophan, as consumers began to learn that it could dramatically improve emotional well being. But, then tragedy struck. A contaminated batch of tryptophan from a Japanese lab that was synthesizing it led to the deaths of approximately thirty people and the severe illness of a thousand more. Instead of finding the source of the problem and making certain that the supply was pure, the FDA attributed the problem to tryptophan and pulled it from the shelves. This draconian measure has, like much bureaucratic ineptitude, become permanent. The result is that tryptophan, as a supplement, although a simple, direct and inexpensive solution to a critical nutritional deficiency is largely unavailable and was made a prescription only drug.

To make matters more complicated, the human body's ability to properly utilize any substance, whether tryptophan or not, also depends on its supply of other nutrients. For example, there is evidence that adequate amounts of vitamin C and certain B vitamins are needed for the process of utilizing tryptophan to work correctly. So, the first step in producing an adequate amount of serotonin is getting enough tryptophan. The next step is supporting your body with proper nutrition so that it can be utilized.

What do we do When we are Low on Serotonin?

Since the human body is a great feedback mechanism, we resort to strategies that have made us feel better in the past when we sense that we are low on serotonin. No, we do not say to ourselves, "Hey, I'm running low on serotonin" and make a run to the nearest laboratory. But, we begin to feel blue or low on emotional energy and, suddenly find ourselves craving those things that make us feel better, or not, or temporarily.

In layman's terms, we head for the carbohydrates. We load up on bread and pasta because they stimulate the release of serotonin in the brain. We do not know this on a conscious level, but we know that we feel better emotionally when we have them. We find ourselves craving sugar and all of its many sources: candy, sodas, pies, pastries and alcohol. One of the symptoms of a person who is low on serotonin is a craving for bread, pasta, and sweets.

As you can imagine, the results of craving carbohydrates to satisfy a serotonin deficiency are long-term health problems: overweight, hypoglycemia, diabetes, low physical energy, and mood swings. Carbohydrate cravings lead to binge eating and eating disorders. To make matters worse, the denatured carbohydrates that are consumed are merely a short-term fix for low serotonin levels. Over the long term, their consumption inhibits the utilization of tryptophan and serotonin by depleting the body of B vitamins. So, it becomes a vicious circle.

Some of the other strategies practiced to overcome serotonin deficiencies are using stimulants, which force the release of other brain chemicals that mask depression, such as adrenaline and beta-endorphins.

1. We smoke because smoking stimulates the production of adrenal hormones that stimulate us. Recent studies showed that people who suffered from depression were actually helped by smoking and that they could become dangerously depressed when they gave up smoking. In other words, they were self-medicating for depression.

2. We become chocoholics. Chocolate has come under considerable study lately for its

chemical properties that can reduce depression. However, the result is temporary and you can develop blood sugar problems as a result.

3. We live on Coke and coffee. The caffeine in these drinks stimulates the release of adrenal hormones.

4. We head for the gym because exercise releases beta-endorphins in our brains that make us feel buoyant and happy while counteracting the ill effects of low serotonin. This is one of the positive strategies although it too can be overdone.

5. We turn to compulsive addictive behaviors that stimulate the production of beta-endorphins.

As you can see, most of these strategies are extremely unproductive for traders. In fact, they are likely to sabotage your career. At the same time that you are resorting to these sabotaging behaviors, you will find yourself trying to stop them and not being able to do so. The reason is that your actions are not being driven on a conscious level, and are therefore, not amenable to reason and self-discipline.

Taking the Cures

The pharmaceutical industry has conveniently benefited from the limitations placed on the individual's access to more natural remedies. This may explain, in part, why the government is so slow to reverse its position on tryptophan. What the pharmaceutical companies have come up with is a host of drugs which, when taken, slow down or inhibit the neutralization in the synapse of serotonin by the monoamine (MAO).

The most popular new drugs for treating depression and mood disorders are called SSRI's or serotonin re-uptake inhibitors. And that is just what they do. They increase the level of serotonin by inhibiting the re-uptake of it in the synapses. You recognize these drugs by name because they have become common household words. Prozac is undoubtedly the most famous.

Here is the problem. In order to stop a chemical reaction, another set of chemicals is added to the mix. We know that the process of turning tryptophan into the right amount of serotonin and then neutralizing it is very complex. If the right mix of other chemicals needed for these reactions is not present, then simply adding serotonin or forcing serotonin levels to remain high by stopping their re-uptake is not enough to make the process work. The result of messing with Mother Nature can be a host of unintended side effects that can range from mild to extreme, depending upon the individual.

Then, there are other problems caused by taking multiple medications. Until recently, no one mentioned the terrible, disabling pain that resulted from mixing serotonin producers and inhibitors at the same time. The condition has become a hot topic on the Internet for the growing number of sufferers. Many of these sufferers have been told by their doctors, who are unaware of the problem, that it is merely a problem of migraines or possibly psychosomatic. But, those unfortunates who live with the permanent results are warning the public not to mix multiple medications.

The Alternatives

The alternatives to Prozac and drugs of its type depend upon the source of the problem. So, just like having your doctor experiment with you to see what works, you will need to be willing to do the same on your own. Here are some possible alternatives:

1. Increasing serotonin through diet. If your diet is sadly deficient in protein (or you don't digest protein well) and the B vitamins and antioxidants, it is possible that you may be able to improve your situation by simply improving your diet.

2. St. John's Wort. The German's have been prescribing the herb, St. John's Wort, for a long time and they have done considerable testing on it to prove that it is efficacious. Why? Because it increases the production of serotonin. They have found it to have very few, if any, side effects. One important caution is that you need to stay out of the sun. But, the good news is that you can buy St. John's Wort at your local supermarket or health food store. We do not yet know whether this alternative is viable for long-term use.

3. 5HTP – Before tryptophan turns into serotonin, there is an intermediate stage called 5HTP, which requires an enzyme that many are deficient in. For many people, taking the compound 5HTP, which you can also buy in a health food store, is more effective than taking tryptophan (and you can take a much lower dose), St. John's Wort, or one of the pharmaceuticals. Unfortunately, since this substance is derived from tryptophan, it is also subject to the possibility that its manufacture can be contaminated. However, it can also be made from an herbal extract from the herb griffonia and is very safe. A problem with contamination developed some time back and many health food stores, fearing a return of the tryptophan catastrophe, pulled their supplies of 5HTP from the shelves. Fortunately, there appear to be a few good sources left and it is possible to locate them through alternative doctors and good health food stores. Like St. John's Wort there is a cautionary warning to avoid taking vitamin B6 within three hours of taking St. John's Wort because it will not work as well. Before you run to your health food store looking for 5HTP, you should check with a medical doctor with an extensive nutritional background or an alternative medical practitioner.

Conclusion

A trader's successful career depends upon his emotional well being. There are plenty of resources that we can rely upon to help us deal with the emotional issues that result from our personal experiences. Now, with the recent research into our brain biochemistry, we have a new set of strategies that can be used when those emotional problems have a physical cause. We are not necessarily limited to taking drugs, but if we do need to take these new mood altering drugs, at least we have an understanding of what they do and why. And finally, we can take a new look at some of the uncomfortable things that are going on in our lives and see possible biochemical reasons so we can take appropriate action. If knowledge is power for the rest of the world, knowledge is money for a trader. And serotonin could be a gold mine.

In part 2 of this series on "Traders and Serotonin," we will continue to explore the things that you can do to increase your emotional and physical well being by increasing the serotonin levels in your brain. In addition, we will look at some of the other neurotransmitters as sources of trouble with your emotional balance. And, we will recommend some books and other resources to assist you.

Chapter 21

TRADERS AND SERONTONIN
PART 2

Recently, I spoke with a trader named John who had read "*Traders and Serotonin, Part One*" and had put into practice what he had read. John had just returned from a trip to his local pharmacy, a trip which marked a turning point in his life.

During John's wait in the crowded store, one computer and one cash register had failed, doctors had been called to confirm prescriptions, insurance companies had declined prescriptions, and countless mistakes had occurred. Finally, John had reached the front of the line and handed his single refilled prescription to the cashier. At that moment, a woman with fifteen prescriptions was allowed to go ahead of him because she had waited longer. Due to technical difficulties that the pharmacy was experiencing, each of her prescriptions required a full minute to ring up. By this time, John had been waiting for over an hour and a half.

If this event had occurred just a few weeks earlier, John would have been boiling with rage by the time he reached the cashier. Then, adding insult to injury by putting the fifteen-prescription transaction in front of him would have blown him over the top. He would have vented his rage at the clerk, the customer, and anyone else in his crosshairs.

Instead, by his account, John stood in line smiling and repeating to himself the magic little formula, "5HTP." This little formula had changed his entire life. Gone were his rages and ensuing depressions. Gone were his frustrations at small inconveniences. Gone, too, were his paranoid perceptions of petty and covert slights, insults and attacks. Now, he sleeps well most nights and awakens with energy and enthusiasm. His moods are no longer pessimistic and negative. He handles the stresses of his job with equanimity.

"I never realized until I started taking the 5HTP how low my serotonin levels actually were," he told me. John's wife, children, dogs, and associates, however, all had an inkling, but he was unable to hear their feedback. By the way, John's trading is the best it has been in a long time.

A Caution

As you know, I am neither a scientist nor a physician. What you are reading about in these two articles is the result of my research and my educated observations and work with countless traders and others in the field. I urge you to do your own reading and research on the subject. At the end of this article, I will give you a short list of books to read. I also urge you to go online and check out the extensive readings available to you there. But, most importantly, if you feel that you need to avail yourself or someone close to you of the various natural and pharmacological treatments available for depression, I urge you to work with a physician who has educated himself extensively in this area. If need be, bring him books and articles to read so that you have a partner in this process. Self-medicating can be as dangerous as skydiving without a chute.

In Part One of this series on depression, we reviewed the effect of depression and low serotonin levels on the professional and personal well being of a trader. We briefly explained the way messages in the brain pass from one neuron to the next by way of little chemical messengers called neurotransmitters. The three major transmitters that affect mood are serotonin, which is most responsible for lifting depression and calming us, while norepinephrine and dopamine are the two neurotransmitters most responsible for stimulation.

As we learned, the high level and/or production of serotonin (and these other neuro-transmitters) is necessary in order to keep the messages transmitted along the neurons, and to keep us from sinking into depression and anxiety.

When we see the problem of low serotonin levels, we want to fix it. The problem with solving a problem in one part of the body is that the human body is highly complex. Each simple interaction can be the final result of millions, if not billions, of other chemical reactions having taken place elsewhere. To repair one reaction at the end of the line may well mean that you are tinkering with reactions that are taking place in very unrelated parts of your body. When we do this, troubles can multiply.

The Prozac Pack and its Problems
The enzyme that neutralizes serotonin (a monoamine) is called monoamine oxidase. To prevent this enzyme from scooping up needed serotonin, scientists have created a set of inhibitors for the inhibitor which they call monoamine oxidase inhibitors or MAOI's and SSRI's, or serotonin reuptake inhibitors. The most famous of these serotonin inhibitors is Prozac. However, Prozac merely leads the pack of the serotonin enhancing drugs, which include: Paxil, Zoloft, Effexor, Remeron, Wellbutrin, Celexa, Serzone, and Luvox. The entire pack should be considered together since they share so many of the same problems.

Why have problems resulted from something as benign as serotonin? First, it is important to understand that only 5% of the serotonin in the body is in the brain. The rest is distributed in the intestinal tract, liver, blood stream, genitals, etc. where it regulates the rhythmic movements of the food, blood flow and clotting, and sexual function. Anything affecting the level of serotonin, is not just going to have an effect on the serotonin in the brain.

Many of the most serious problems are a result of the fact that serotonin is a member of a team with the other neurotransmitters. Together, they maintain a delicate chemical balance in the brain. Specifically, dopamine and serotonin have a special interdependent relationship that can be viewed like a seesaw. When they are in balance, they are at the same level, but if one is elevated, the other drops off proportionately. The serotonin enhancers actually boost serotonin to artificially high levels beyond what they would be normally.

When the reuptake of serotonin occurs naturally, the process keeps the signal crisp by preventing any lingering serotonin from hanging around. Once that process is halted and serotonin stays in the synapse, this creates hyper-stimulation that triggers "compensatory" reaction in the other transmitters. In this case, dopamine levels drop off, which can result in some very serious complications. No one really understood this relationship when these serotonin enhancers first came onto the market. Unfortunately, the backlash from dopamine has severe consequences, with silent and progressive brain damage that is often not evident until it has become severe. With no effective, long-term monitoring policy in place, the public has been performing the role of test subject on these drugs.

1. Life Threatening Problems

- **Strokes**
  What we did not tell you is that the enzyme, monoamine oxidase, that scoops up serotonin in the brain and which Prozac and its cousins are designed to inhibit, is also present in the liver and the intestines. So, if inhibiting this enzyme in the brain is a good thing because it makes more serotonin available, it can be a very bad thing in the liver and intestines. When monamine oxidase is not present in the intestine, the result is the panicky release of norepinephrine into the bloodstream. Suddenly, your blood pressure shoots up dangerously sending you toward a life-threatening stroke.

  Unfortunately, there are a host of foods that can trigger this reaction: aged cheeses, bottled and on-tap beer, anchovies, broad beans, liver, overripe bananas, pickled meats, soy sauce, red and white wine (except Chianti.) This means that when you begin taking these serotonin enhancers, you also have to go on a special diet, and stick to it or pay the consequences.

- **Suicidal and Homicidal Compulsions**
  Although, this is not a common reaction to these drugs, these frightening reactions are a well-documented side effect. Unfortunately, there is no way to know in advance who is going to react in this manner. The initial scare about this reaction was quelled by the drug companies and then managed by prescribing smaller initial dosages. However, the danger still persists.

141

2. Tics, Abnormal Movements

Facial tics, involuntary body movements, cud-chewing, tongue-darting, lip-smacking, leg-tapping, muscle spasms, and Parkinsonism (symptoms like Parkinson's Disease - including extreme exhaustion, slowed movements, diminished facial movement and eventual immobilization) are common side effects of these drugs. Some of these tics disappear over time, but some remain as evidence of permanent brain damage, depending upon how long the dosage was given. At 60 years old, the average person has lost 40% of the cells in the region specific to Parkinson's disease, whereas the person with Parkinson's Disease has lost 80%. If, having been on Prozac for an extended period results in an additional and significant loss of cells in this region, what is the long-term prognosis for this individual? There is some evidence that this is a serious threat.

3. Drug Interactions

Monoamine oxidase suppressors and serotonin enhancers may conflict with other drugs in very dangerous ways. Thus, you cannot mix two of these anti-depressants because of the danger of an overproduction of serotonin. This overdose would cause a rapid heartbeat, high blood pressure, hyperactivity and possible seizures. You must also not take appetite or cough suppressants, decongestants, drugs for asthma or allergies.

Illegal drugs that are addictive such as cocaine, metamphetamines, and heroin are very dangerous to take also since they are also enhancers of brain neurotransmitters and are known to raise dopamine levels. A new illegal drug, Ectasy, creates a surge of serotonin.

4. Sexual Dysfunction

From 60-75% of patients on Prozac experience sexual dysfunction and become sexually impotent or lose all interest in sex, or experience vaginal anesthesia, retrograde or delayed ejaculation.

5. Memory Loss

Zoloft in particular seems to have a pattern of causing memory loss. After stopping the drug, this symptom generally disappears.

6. Weight Rebounding

Many people discover that they lose weight in the first year on these drugs, only to gain weight rapidly back thereafter.

7. Drug Dependency and "Wear Off"

Like addictive drugs, actual drug dependency can occur and the effect of these drugs can "wear off," requiring progressively higher doses for the same results.

8. Withdrawal

Like addictive drugs, these serotonin enhancers can have devastating withdrawal symptoms which commonly include:

- Electric shocks that shoot through your body - these are very powerful and frightening
- Dizziness, spinning sensations, and visual disturbances
- Sleep disorders
- Gastrointestinal disorders including vomiting and nausea
- Flu-like symptoms
- Rages and/or irritable outbursts, smashing things and punching walls
- Suicidal and homicidal reactions
- Other side effects: Insomnia, dizziness, constipation, rapid heartbeat and blood pressure that is too low or too high

SAM-e - A Friend in Need is a Friend Indeed

The newest and possibly the most effective, and certainly the fastest-acting of the more natural treatments for depression is called SAM-e. Known to the European market since the early 1980's, SAM-e did not enter the American market until 1998. It was introduced by the Italian company, Knoll SPa, which holds the patent on it. Knoll SPa's parent company BASF licensed three American companies to market SAM-e in the States in 1999. Because of the 1994 Dietary and Supplement Health and Education Act, which permitted the public access to herbal and natural products without extensive drug testing, SAM-e is available to anyone in America on the shelves of health food stores. In Europe it is available only by prescription.

What is SAM-e?

S-adenosylmethione (or SAM-e) is a naturally occurring compound in the body which decreases in production as we age. It is present in most cells and is essential for the production of countless vital processes in the body. SAM-e results from combination of the amino acid methionine and adenosine triphosphate (ATP). These compounds are essential to the production of energy and a process called methylation and another one called trans-sulfuration.

This first process, methylation, has a profound impact on the brain, One of the most important roles of SAMe is to improve and increase the level of methylation. In turn, methylation increases the transmission of the chemical messages from serotonin and the other neurotransmitters, thus improving the level of your moods. Then, methylation aids in the production of acetycholine, a neurotransmitter than peps you up and helps you to retain information. Finally, methylation makes the walls of the nerve cells pliable and permeable so that neuro-messages can get through. Because of its vital role in methylation, SAM-e is able to work rapidly to counteract depression, unlike the MAOI's and SSRI's which can take three weeks to begin to show their effects.

Through trans-sulfuration, SAM-e can become the precursor to the powerful antioxidant, glutathione, which protects the lenses of your eyes and detoxifies the liver, among other things. This important process requires the presence of Vitamin B6 in order to work.

As a byproduct of its various chemical reactions in the body, SAM-e also turns into homocysteine, a compound which, in excess, can create heart disease. Although SAM-e creates homocysteine, it does not do so in a way that is dangerous to the body, Instead, it turns around and then stimulates the process of eliminating homocysteine by turning it back into mehionine through remethylation. But remethylation requires not only SAM-e but the two B vitamins, folic acid and B12 to occur. Interestingly enough, depressed people tend to have lowered levels of these B vitamins. However, taking these B vitamins and the amino acid methionine do not seem to help increase methylation. Only taking the SAM-e seems to have a positive effect.

What are the Functional Benefits of Taking SAM-e?

1. First, SAM-e is a highly effective and rapid reducer of depression by allowing serotonin and the other neurotransmitters to move more freely.

2. It protects the cell membranes through the processes of methylation and trans-sulfuration.

3. It is an effective, safe treatment for arthritis. SAM-e helps the body to produce glucosamine sulphate and chondroitin, substances that are known to produce the shock-absorbing tissue in your joints. The level of these naturally occurring compounds in your body begin to decline in your forties and the loss of them can result in the painful arthritic symptoms that begin at that stage life.

4. Through its effect on complex chemical reactions, it helps to regulate DNA

5. It helps repair liver damage due to excessive drinking and hepatitis

6. It appears to help with Parkinson's Disease and Alzheimer's Disease

7. It protects the lenses of your eyes

8. It reduces inflammation.

What are the Side Benefits of Taking SAM-e?

1. Very few side effects. It does not have the mild but unpleasant side effects of the MAOI'S and the SSRI's such as headaches, dry mouth, fogginess, anxiety, insomnia, or the serious side effects of sexual dysfunction, severe low or high blood pressure, unwanted weight gains or losses.

2. Does not require a prescription

3. It acts rapidly - reputably twice as fast as the best pharmaceuticals and six times as fast as St. John's Wort

4. You can stay on it as long as you want

Here are Some Important Things to Know About Taking SAM-e:

Which Individuals Should Take it?
- The depressed with low mood and low energy who want immediate relief and have not been helped by any other treatment
- The elderly
- The arthritic
- The long-term depressed who need long-term treatment
- Alcoholics and people with liver disease - people who have consumed too much alcohol in their lives have clear deficiencies of SAM-e and are missing the enzyme that turns methionine into SAM-e
- People looking for a more natural treatment

Which Individuals Should NOT Take it?
- Manic-depressives - In these individuals, SAM-e can lead to manic episodes
- People with panic or anxiety disorders- in these people, SAM-e may make their hearts race, leading to a feeling of panic
- Anyone currently taking MAO inhibitors or SSRI's- it takes several weeks for these drugs to work their way out of the system and the withdrawal must be monitored by a physician.

How to Buy SAM-e:
- The cost of SAM-e can range from $.87 per pill to $2.71 per pill depending on the source, so shopping around is a good idea.
- You must be certain that your source is a good one, so if you do not buy one of the sources that is licensed by Knoll SPa, you should check out the source in *The SAM-e Handbook* by Nancy Steadman, M.S., published in 2000 by The Three Rivers Press, NY.
- Check with your nutritionist for reputable brands. Some of the options are Nature Made, GNC, Nuttralife, and Solgar.

Stress and Serotonin

We seem to continually return to stress and its effect on our health and well being. In the case of depression and serotonin levels, there is new evidence to suggest that the problem with serotonin is just another way-station in the search for the underlying causes of depression. Yes, we know that some people are simply missing the enzymes needed to maintain the level of serotonin in the brain. However, there is reason to believe that there are stress-related causes that go deeper in the problem for many of the sufferers of depression - stress may be the primary cause of depression while the level of serotonin (and other neurotransmitters may be the secondary cause.) One of the reasons for this hypothesis is the fact that the level of these neurotransmitters can rise and fall without immediately changing mood.

Studies show that depressed people tend to have elevated levels of the adrenal stress hormone cortisol in their blood, thus keeping them in a continued state of stress. Further evidence shows that the adrenal gland is enlarged in a third of the people who are suffering from depression.

The chain reaction that gets this all started is a stressful episode - one that we perceive as stressful. In the brain, the hypothalamus reacts to this stimulus by sending a message to the pituitary. This message comes in the form of a hormone called CRH (corticotropin-releasing hormone) which in turn sends a message to the adrenals. The adrenals, in turn, shoot out the stress hormones adrenaline or epinephrine to put you in a state of fight or flight.

Is it possible that the continued presence of cortisol in the bloodstream could be damaging in some way to the receptors for serotonin or to the enzymes that are vital to the process of production and reuptake? We already know that the presence of cortisol is damaging to memory in the brain. People who have been through a traumatic event, especially one that is of long duration are now known to lose memory permanently.

The Old Panacea

Although the triggers for stress can be one-time traumatic events, the day-to-day stresses that have no solutions can keep us in a continued state of adrenal alert. No drug can cure this situation without causing a host of other problems. The only viable, healthy way to reduce the stress that we actually experience is through meditation. The method proposed by the Harvard doctors in the book, *The Relaxation Response*, has been scientifically studied and proven to reduce or eliminate the flight or flight response during the day. Although the studies were conducted to show the reduction in blood pressure and heart disease, the thousands of years of observation in the East have demonstrated the effect of the right kind of meditation on mood and mental health.

A Balanced Life

It is interesting to see that in order for SAM-e to perform its vital work in the body, it requires three B vitamins: B6, folic acid, and B12. When stress occurs in the body and the adrenal glands are required to produce adrenal hormones, it must have B6, B2, and pantothenic acid as well as vitamin C in order to manufacture its hormones. Continued stress depletes the bodies store of these vitamins, while alcohol, sugar and white flour consumption deplete B2 and B6, pantothenic acid and thiamine and niacine, as well as most of the other B vitamins. For that reason, one could make the case that good nutrition is just as effective in fighting depression as a good MAOI or SSRI like Prozac.

Forty years ago, Adelle Davis began writing books on nutrition and talked about the nutritional science of depression. Her writings are beginning to look like cutting edge material all over again as she stressed foods rich in B vitamins and fish oils. We now know that Omega 3 fatty acids present in fish and fish oils have a role in regulating levels of brain serotonin. In countries where the people eat a lot of fish, the levels of major depression and postpartum depression are low. Omega 3 fatty acids positively affect the signals in the brain synapses by changing the shape of the membranes making it easier for the neurotransmitters to bind.

We touched briefly on exercise in Part One of this article. I would like to mention again that exercise is a healthy way to deal with depression. Runner's high is a well-known phenomenon and can lift a depressed spirit. Regular exercise should be part of a regimen for mental health just as much as it should be for your physical well being. For example, ninety minutes on a treadmill actually doubles the levels of serotonin in the brain!

A balanced life also includes the enjoyment of your environment, including the arts. The ancient Greeks first developed the concept of music therapy. Since music is experienced in the limbic system of the brain, music can release endorphins, which counteract depression and create a sense of joy. The iso-moodic method of reducing depression has you match the music you listen to with your existing mood and gradually shift toward the music that matches the mood you desire.

And, finally, I'd like to put in a word for sleep and maintaining a routine. Studies show that going to bed at the same time each night and awakening the same time each morning has a positive effect on your emotional health. Once you figure out whether you are an owl and can get to bed late or a lark and need to get to bed early, you should stick to your routine. Upsetting that routine can trigger depression and mood swings.

Some Books to Read

I would like to recommend the following books on the subject of serotonin and depression. Each one contains valuable information:

1. *Dealing with Depression Naturally: Complementary and Alternative Therapies for Restoring Emotional Health* by Syd Baumel (Excellent review of alternative treatments,)
2. *Serotonin* by Syd Baumel (Everything you need to know about Serotonin)
3. *Prozac Backlash: Overcoming the Dangers of Prozac, Zoloft, Paxil, and other Antidepressants with Safe, Effective Alternatives*, by Joseph Glenmullen, M.D.(You'll never take a serotonin enhancer after reading this book.)
4. *Molecules of Emotion: the Science behind Mind-Body Medicine* by Candace B. Pert, Ph.D. (This book includes an extensive list of mind body treatment centers)
5. *The Biology of Success* by Robert Arnot, M.D. (This book contains a wealth of specific natural therapies, self-tests, and resources)
6. *The SAM-e Handbook: The Fast, Natural Way to Overcome Depression, Relieve the Pain of Arthritis, Alleviate the Discomfort of Fibromyalgia, and Boost Your Energy* By Nancy Stedman (Everything you need to know about SAM-e and how to get it)

Conclusion

We have just scraped the surface of this very important issue for traders. At this very moment, scientists and people in the medical field all around the globe are uncovering revolutionary information about the biochemistry of our emotions and how we can use that information to reduce our episodes of depression and anxiety. What we know is that our moods are affected by the levels of specific neurotransmitters that work together in a delicate balance in our brain and in our body. In order to feel better, think better, and perform better in the world of the markets, we must take care of ourselves, and educate ourselves, while looking for the safest, most natural, and healthiest ways to enhance our "mind-body" well being.

Chapter 22

_____

DEALING WITH DISTRACTIONS

For investors or traders to make important money-risking decisions, they must possess the ability to focus on the important tasks at hand. To focus, you must have a quiet place where only you, your rules, and the execution of an opportunity exist. This formula sounds simple. But, in the Twenty-First Century, we live with myriad distractions that enter our lives on a second-by-second basis. Distractions arrive through our mailboxes, over our televisions, by way of our cellular telephones and, of course, "You've got mail." With this chaos surrounding us, it can feel miraculous when we do make intelligent, profitable decisions. For most investor/traders, the problem of distractions is even worse when you are working from home than if you are investing and trading from an out-of-the-home office. That is the reason I have listed the five most common distractions and strategies for handling them.

The Biggest Distraction

The biggest distraction to sound decision-making in investing/trading is your own self-talk. Of course, this distraction is present at your office, but it is even more intrusive when you are in your own environment and surrounded by all of the cues that can trigger thoughts about the problems and issues in your life. Your self-talk is that voice in your head that interprets everything that you are feeling and doing and everything that is happening around you. Self-talk can be positive, as in "That was a really good decision," or it can be negative, as in, "How could I have been such a fool?" While other people are talking to you, self-talk can be running in your head at about 125 words per minute. But, when they stop, it can hit top speeds of up to 400 words a minute. If your self-talk is filled with a lot of emotion, it can be very, very distracting.

Imagine that you are investing with a money manager. If you could hear his self-talk, and he is saying, "Maybe I should wait on this trade, suppose it goes against me, suppose I lose money on this trade, I know it will come back!" Would you want this person to handle your money? Of course not, you would pull your account very quickly from a so-called money manager who thought in this way. But the fact is you are letting your investments be handled by a money manager who thinks like that and that individual is you. When you engage in negative, conflicting self-talk, you distract yourself from making sound decisions. Trading/investing cannot be profitable if you are not willing to look at the big picture of winning. This big picture is the motivator toward positive thoughts and actions. You might lose a battle or two along the way to making money, but you will never win the war if your thought distractions prevent you from taking action.

Dealing with Self-Talk

Notice what you are saying to yourself and when you are saying it:
Example:

- **What are you saying?** "Ah, a good opportunity but is it a false signal? I'll wait a bit. Should have taken it before. Maybe it's too late. No, it's still a good opportunity. But suppose it reverses itself? Better wait for the next opportunity. Oops, should have taken that one. I would have made $6,000."
- **When are you saying it?** Is it first thing in the morning or later in the day?
- **Are you comfortable with the risk you are taking?**

Strategies for Dealing with Self-Talk

1. If you took all of your money-making opportunities, what would the results be?
   - If the results were positive, remember that many good methodologies lose at least 50% of the time and you say to yourself:
     - "All opportunities in my methodology will lead me to a win."
     - If you do not believe you will make money, proceed to Strategy #2.

2. If you were to take only 50% of the best opportunities, what would the results be? (This could be any percentage)
   - If the results would be positive, say to yourself:
     - "I feel confident that when I take ____ % of my opportunities, I have predetermined that the probabilities of making money are in my favor."
     - If your analysis does not have a profitable outcome, go back to the drawing board and rework your rules.

3. If your negative self-talk occurs mostly in the morning, you need to prepare more either the night before or earlier in the day. Run through scenarios to mentally rehearse taking signals as a result of positive thinking. In addition, low adrenal function can prevent you from sleeping properly and can lead to a feeling of exhaustion and hopelessness as you begin your day.

4. If your negative thinking occurs late in the day, you could be tired and your neurology could be protecting you from making wrong choices. Take time during the day to rejuvenate by taking a short nap or meditating.

5. How much are you risking at any given opportunity? Are you comfortable with that risk?

You might want to adjust your risk based on how you feel about the probabilities of the investment going in a profitable direction. Regardless of your risk choices, they must be based on your predetermined criteria. It is important to be consistent. Consistency gives you a base for improving your criteria for opportunities. Negative self-talk is your way of protecting yourself when you are not comfortable about the risk you are taking. If you cannot handle risk, give your money to someone who can, employ a coach, or give up investing.

But It's Ringing!

Did you ever notice how people give immediate priority to a ringing telephone over anything else that is happening in their lives? How many calls are actually that important for us to answer? Not many. Should answering the telephone take priority over making important decisions about your money? It is interesting how most people complain about interruptions from telephone solicitors, relatives, friends and associates when it is unlikely that there is an emergency, but they still continue to answer the telephone immediately when it rings.

Strategies for Dealing with the Phone
Sometimes the most obvious actions for improvement must be stated to make the changes, so here goes:
1. Let your answering machine screen calls.
2. Ask people not to call during certain times, unless it is an emergency.
3. Have two separate telephone numbers:
   - The first number is for everyone, including telephone solicitors.
   - The second number is only for those whom you need or want to hear from and who respect your time. If a telephone solicitor is calling you on this line, you usually can hear a click and relevant noises in the background. Just say, "Sorry, no solicitation" or simply hang up. Solicitors are usually on a rotary dialing system and move on to the next call.
4. Arrange for someone else to screen your calls.

Honey, It's Just 10 Minutes

Your spouse is running to the store, the school, or the neighbors, shouting from the door as you hear the rattle of keys, "Honey, would you take care of the baby for ten minutes?" or "Honey, could you entertain the guys while I run out for ten minutes to buy some beer?" Ten-minute requests always seem to come at the same time as an opportunity for making money. And, the time spent is very seldom ten minutes. After all, you don't really have a job, so why should it be a big deal for you to take the time to help someone out for ten minutes? This is how many people view traders/investors who work from home.

Here are some more 10-minute distractions. I'm sure you can identify with them:

- Your mom just dropped by and wants to say "hello."
- The kids want to ask a question about their homework assignment.
- The cat just wants to love you.
- Your husband just wants a kiss.
- Your daughter needs you to 'baby-sit' the grandchildren for the morning.

Aren't these excuses all good reasons for taking breaks from the task of making choices in your investments?

Dealing with the 10-Minute Time-Grabbers

1. Have a meeting with the people in your life who are the potential time-grabbers.
2. Share your goals with them and tell them what cooperation you need from them.
3. Establish your rules for interruptions. Put a sign on your door that lets them know that you are at work and are not to be disturbed unless there is an emergency.
4. If you prefer to keep your door open, arrange hand signals that indicate when you will get back to them or how involved you are.
5. Reward the people who support you in following your rules. For example, provide attentive time later or a special dinner at their favorite pizza place at the end of the week. Make sure you thank them often for their cooperation.

The People in the Know

All day long, interruptions arrive in the form of predictions, suggestions, tips and announcements on the television, on the computer, and in the mail from authorities supposedly making money in the markets. How could you possibly ignore them? They are there to help, guide and give you the best advice available. After all, they have access to more knowledge and better technology than you do. Who are you to disregard their advice? Who are you to make your own decisions?

Dealing with the So-Called Experts

1. If what you receive in the mail, see on television, or any other outside influences tend to take you off course, save it for the end of the day or avoid as many of the outside influences as you can.
2. If you need to use some of this outside information, have someone screen it for you and only look at what you need and want.
3. If you do take advice from an authority that you trust, run the advice through your own criteria for making choices. Remember, in the final analysis, you are responsible for your own decisions and results.

Environmental Attractions

Is the refrigerator beckoning? Are clean-up and organizational projects screaming for attention? Do your other businesses demand attention? Is the sun shining just to get you out on the golf course? When you are bored, unhappy, or unsure of yourself, everything will take priority over your investing/trading.

Strategies for Dealing with Environmental Attractions
1. First, you need a business plan!
2. Next, you need a monthly plan that organizes all of the activities in your life. Make certain that you give attention to all of your activities. It is important to stick with your plan as much as you possibly can. The more you stick with your plan, the more your neurological system and the people around you will support you.

If you do not enjoy the process of making money, you must either develop a strategy for enjoying it or give it up. Otherwise, you will sabotage your efforts.

Conclusion

You can allow any of the countless distractions in your life to draw your attention away from the tasks at hand. However, if you plan and manage these potential distractions with some of the guidelines I have listed, you will not only be able to manage them but yourself, as well. This exercise is a good one to use when developing the discipline necessary to become a top investor/trader.

Chapter 23

_____

WHAT A TRADER MUST KNOW ABOUT ERGONOMICS

Is There No End to Sabotage in Trading?

You've been doing consistently well as a trader sticking to your system, keeping your life in balance, and actually enjoying your work. Then, for no apparent reason you start making decisions that don't make sense. All the old sabotage indicators don't apply any more. The signs are there, but you don't recognize them. So, what are these new signs?

Your Mama Never Told You about "Ergonomics"

Remember when you power off your computer at night, push back your expensive chair and start to get up and feel ten years older than you should? Your shoulders and neck ache, your thighs feel numb, and your lower back is stiff and sore. While these symptoms are merely irritants now, if you don't attend to them, they will almost surely get worse. You need serious help with ergonomics.

According to the Department of Labor, ergonomics is "the study of work" or more broadly, "the science of designing the job to fit the worker." Ergonomics as a topic caught the public's eye in the 1970's when OSHA began to cite companies for a dramatic increase in muscular-skeletal disorders. While the discipline covers subjects from psychology to labor relations, a trader needs to concern himself primarily with data acquired from its health sciences and engineering facets.

Muscular-skeletal Disorders (MSD's) are injuries to or disorders of the soft tissues and nervous system. These tissues include muscles, tendons, ligaments, joints and cartilage. Many of these injuries are Repetitive Strain Injuries (RSI's) where muscles, nerves or tendons become irritated or inflamed by actions that in isolation would be harmless. Other MSD's can cause symptoms ranging from numbness and stiff joints to muscle loss, constant long-term pain, and sometimes paralysis. Traders who work non-ergonomically are more likely to succumb to these afflictions.

The potential for certain harms are inherent in the trader's work and environment. Improper keyboard placement or operation can cause carpal tunnel syndrome with its tingling, numbness, severe pain, and loss of strength in the hands and wrists or tendonitis with its pain and swelling in fingers or wrists resulting from inflammation of the tendons. Repeated use of the index finger, as with a mouse, can cause difficulty moving the finger in snapping or jerking movements.

Back pain is a catch all phrase for a condition that will affect eight out of ten Americans in their lifetimes. Since our spines didn't evolve very well, we tend to have problems with our backs anyway. Poor ergonomics and the stress of trading combine to cause additional back problems. With your spine twisted and the muscles of your lower back bunched incorrectly in your chair, you are a sitting duck for that moment of tension when you give a little twist and "BAM!" You've got a lower back strain. You may be jolted by spasms, unable to move, or you may be bent double. The strain may be on one side of the spine or both and the spasms may even keep you awake at night. The prescription for treatment is usually complete bed rest for one to three days. However, traders usually choose to stay in pain and gulp pain relievers and wonder why they have just sabotaged their trading results.

Examining the Past and Present

Sometimes a trader needs ergonomics to prevent the worsening of a pre-existing condition such as a herniated disk. Weight gain, long hours, and increased tension can cause a trader's once adequate office setup to aggravate his condition. When this occurs, the trader needs to think about how the use of his office can help him instead of hurting him. Disk problems, for instance, need to be taken care of on several fronts. As sufferers know, disk problems can lead to surgery or ever more desperate attempts seeking relief from the nagging pain.

A trader who is slumping down into his chair has altered the angle of his head to the screen and his arms to the keyboard. He has unknowingly set himself up for shoulder muscle strain and neck strain. These ailments can cause anything from soreness and stiffness, which is usually alleviated with damp heat, to spasms, cramping and severe pain, making work impossible for a time. If these symptoms are ignored, more serious and long-lasting ailments can replace them such as shoulder tendonitis or bursitis.

Finally, poor ergonomics can hurt your legs. Improper placement of feet on the floor can restrict blood flow, which will damage muscles and tendons. Numbness, weakness, or tingling down one leg is called sciatica and is caused by a pinched nerve in the lower back. Leg numbness can also be the sign of a serious illness and should not be ignored if it persists.

If you experience any of these problems, and you think your office situation may be a contributing factor, you need to do some office reorganization. First, stand in the doorway and take a fresh look around. The room itself should look comfortable to you. When considering the placement of the desk, hopefully some outside light will be available to the area. Your work area should not be cluttered or glum. If there is no greenery to see out of the window, often a few low-maintenance, low-light plants to the side of the work area can create the right balance.

Do You Have Enough Chair?

Once you've completed moving furniture, the best place to start is an ergonomic assessment of your chair. Speaking of the chair, didn't that salesman mention ergonomics when he sold it to you with all of its bells and whistles? You bought it because it sat well. Now it's time to check out the bells and whistles. Ideally, your chair should have a stable base using five legs with casters designed for the type of floor that you have: bare or carpeted. Otherwise, casters can roll you away from your position while seated or force you to push them out of ruts in the carpet as you try to rise.

It is important for the chair to have height and tilt adjustment. You should be able to move the seat from about 15 inches to 20 inches from the top of the seat pan to the floor. Should you be much taller or shorter than average, you may need a wider range of adjustment, but if you already have a chair, try to adjust it so that the keyboard is at elbow level. Preferably, the seat pan has the ability to be tilted both forward and backward about 10 degrees. If your chair has this feature, incline the seat pan slightly forward to transfer some of the pressure from the spine to the thighs and feet.

Other Ergonomically Appropriate Features Should Include:
1. A curved seat edge in front with a "waterfall" effect to remove any artificial lift from your thighs.

2. An adjustable back support as to both height and forward and backward tilt. It is important that the backrest support the lower part of the back.

3. A freely rotating swivel, so you can turn easily to side areas of your workstation.

4. Fully adjustable and padded armrests that do not interfere with other chair adjustments or with getting close to your desk.

Adjusting your Work Surface

Ideally, you want to be able to adjust the height of your work surface. If you can do this, you may have already done it in the process of adjusting your chair. The basic dynamic between the chair and desk is that your elbows are at right angles to the work surface and your forearms are parallel to the floor, making your fingers level with keyboard. If you cannot create this arrangement because of your chair or desk, then you may have to replace one or the other, unless you can come up with another solution. Sometimes an adjustable keyboard can help.

Monitoring your Monitor

Glare, high contrast, reflections, flicker, dirt and dust will interfere with what you see on the screen and with your effectiveness. Glare and reflection destroy the effectiveness of your screen and should be avoided at all costs. Try positioning your screen at a right angle to your window. If this doesn't work, try tilting the screen to adjust it so there is no glare. You do not want your screen to be below your direct eye level, which will put you into an emotional mode (another form of sabotaging trading.) If the problem persists, you may have to move the monitor. You can try checking overhead lights or even shiny surfaces. Finally, you can try an anti-glare filter or screen hood.

Keep a comfortable viewing distance from the screen, usually 18 to 30 inches. When viewing or typing, your head should not be tilted forward more than 15 degrees. Avail yourself of the variety of text sizes, text styles, and brightness and contrast levels to make creating a document most comfortable for you.

Keying in to Ergonomic Keyboard Use

Avoid unnecessary stress on tendons and muscles in your hands, wrists and forearms. Remember that it takes very little pressure from your fingers to activate the keys of a good keyboard. Some keyboard trays are adjustable, making it possible to align forearms, wrists and hands when the chair and desk are not adjustable. Further, research has shown that there may be less muscle tension in shoulders and forearms when the keyboard is tilted away from you. Also, don't bend your wrists sideways, move your entire hand and forearm over to use the function keys or numeric keypad.

Putting You Back in the Chair

Now that your office is rearranged and everything is adjusted, all you have to do is sit up and lean against the backrest of your chair. Your chair should keep you erect or angled slightly forward. Your arms should be relaxed and loose with your elbows close to your sides and forearms on a straight line with fingers on the keyboard. Your wrists should be as straight as possible on the mouse or trackball. Your thighs should be horizontal to the floor or angled slightly downward, and your feet should be flat on the floor. The torso should remain forward and your head level or tilted only slightly forward.

Conclusion

Obviously, ergonomics is not intended to be a static system that freezes an individual into certain positions. Not every rule will apply to every person exactly, but in applying the standards you will become more aware of what works for you. Ergonomics is also about relaxation. Find a series of desk stretches, try them carefully, and then use them whenever you feel the need. Look away from the screen at intervals that you find relaxing. Experiment to find your most effective work and break dynamic and try to follow a schedule. You've spent the time to adjust your workspace and your work habits. Should you experience wrist pain or backache, you will be able to take a watchful position or make some sensible adjustments in your life. Finally, if your problem of sabotage and/or tension persists, after a reasonable time you'll have the wisdom to see your health care professional or trading coach.

Chapter 24

_____

DO YOU HAVE COMPUTER VISION SYNDROME?

But It's Only Eyestrain

Jack has taken the time to upgrade his office so that everything is ergonomically correct. His chair, desk, and monitor are placed so that when he sits before his workstation, he is in an accurate work position. He is attentive to his posture, takes occasional breaks, and does occasional stretches. But, even with this attention to ergonomic detail, the muscles of his upper back, neck and shoulders are very tired and sore before his workday ends. What has caused Jack's pain and made his afternoon effectiveness take a nosedive? Surprisingly, Jack is the victim of eyestrain.

Considered an annoyance by most traders, eyestrain is one of a group of interrelated eye problems caused or exacerbated by computer use and called Computer Vision Syndrome (CVS.) CVS is an umbrella term for anything from Jack's almost unnoticeable irritation to the much more serious eye problem known as "age-related macular degeneration." Even simple eyestrain, which is usually characterized by blurred vision, eye dryness, or excess tearing, may not be as harmless as it seems. Eye muscle movement is involuntary, but often a trader will use voluntary muscles in the face, neck, and shoulders, in an attempt to keep working with eyestrain. This is what has been happening to Jack. As his vision begins to blur toward the end of his day, he leans forward, craning his neck and even hunching his shoulders in an attempt to see better.

To get the real effect of Jack's shift from good to dismal posture, imagine a spot of tiny script in the center of your computer screen. To read this script, you must lean forward to within 12 inches of the screen and squint. Notice how your torso, neck and even shoulders re-position when this is attempted for a short time. Now, imagine pulling and twisting these muscles in an attempt to see different parts of the screen for an extended period of time.

Jack assumes that his dry eyes and blurred vision are of no more consequence than his foot being asleep. Because he discounts the significance of his symptoms and it is late in the day, he is actually unaware of his posture shift. He also pushes the muscle aches aside until he is through for the day. That is when he finally becomes completely aware of his stiff neck and the dull ache in his lower back with headache and sore shoulders. Even a soothing dip in the hot tub fails to completely relieve his pain or relax him. Jack doesn't understand what has happened to him because he is unaware of his late afternoon shift in posture. Even with all of his ergonomic office equipment, he is a sitting duck for the accompanying muscle strain when eyestrain kicks in. When muscles are tired, twisting them into awkward positions will only cause additional stress on them. This stress results in the small nerve pinches and muscle tears that create worse muscle problems down the road. As you can see, eyestrain can strain much more than your eyes.

Recent research has determined that computer users blink at 1/3 of the normal blink rate. This could explain several of the initial symptoms of eyestrain: dry eyes with a compensating tearing reaction, itchy eyes, simple eye irritation, uncomfortable contact lenses, and blurred vision. Here are some simple methods to alleviate these eyestrain symptoms: use doctor-recommended artificial tears, eliminate or diminish the flow of air past your eyes, increase the humidity and decrease the contaminants in your office. Make a conscious effort to blink more and concentrate on blinking whenever you start to feel eye discomfort. If you have an eyestrain problem, try to address it before it affects you. At least hourly, close your eyes, breathe deeply, relax your face and roll your eyes around beneath your lids for about 30 seconds. It will work even better if this is done every ten or fifteen minutes. As an added bonus, you may even think about work during this time if you must. Hopefully Jack's story has demonstrated that trying to work with eyestrain can be counterproductive. As a trader, you know that anything emotionally, socially or physically discomforting can negatively affect your work.

Eyestrain and the Serious Stuff

Research has hinted that persistent eyestrain can contribute to more serious vision problems. Researchers on eye disorders are vague about the causes of serious eye disease except where a causal connection has been proved. Time and again, the issues of UV lighting, the symptoms of eyestrain, and an unhealthy atmosphere for eyes are mentioned as potential contributors to these severe disorders. Even symptoms of glaucoma, which include tearing, loss of vision field, and inter-ocular pressure, sound suspiciously similar to symptoms of computer eyestrain. Two disorders are worthy of further discussion.

Visual Form Dysfunction is a disorder caused by an inaccurate eye to brain connection. Often starting in childhood, its origin has been diagnosed as stress to the eyes caused by close work, which certainly fits the description of computer eyestrain. The disorder can be very subtle and can remain undetected for years, because its most obvious symptom is the inability to get the right meaning from small, densely packed material, such as words. A person with this affliction, let's say a trader, may have been an intelligent child who had trouble learning to read and, thus, still has trouble understanding what he has read. Diagnosis can be missed for years because the victim usually has 20/20 vision. Once discovered, training can usually improve the problem. Adults can certainly acquire this condition, and it is not known whether eyestrain will exacerbate it if it is already present.

Do You Need Special Computer Glasses?

A widespread error that seasoned traders are making these days is not getting special computer glasses. Traders of any age should get their eyes checked at least annually and more often if they experience any eye discomfort. Young, nearsighted traders may not need special glasses for their computer monitors because their eyes retain the ability to adjust focus between close objects and very close objects.

Presbyopia, the age-related loss of the ability to change focus of the eye for near viewing, occurs gradually in all adults. Its onset begins in early middle age, and by the time an individual is sixty, this accommodation has effectively been reduced to zero. The usual treatment is reading glasses or multi-focal lenses. As a person gets older, the distance between the eyes and viewing surface becomes more important and this should be a key factor in lens design. The point here is that at some point, most traders will need glasses specifically adapted to the distance between their eyes and the screen.

Jack finally connects his muscular discomfort and drop off in afternoon effectiveness with his mild eyestrain. So, he goes to get his eyes checked. He has been mildly farsighted since high school and has always used reading glasses. Further, he has always used these glasses successfully with the computer screen. It is unlikely that he will realize that he may need glasses designed especially for his positioning at his computer. While the ophthalmologist may be a good diagnostician, he may not ask his patient if he needs the glasses for computer work. If the doctor assumes that the lenses are for page reading, he will likely use the standard testing distance of 16 inches. But Jack, an ergonomics fan, sits between 24 and 26 inches from his computer screen. As a result of missed communication, our trader walks out of the lens shop with glasses that will help him read the newspaper, but will leave him squinting and hunching in front of his computer screen again.

When he visits a new ophthalmologist, Jack discovers that his problem is the beginnings of Presbyopia. Now, he needs to consider his options. With a bifocal fit, such things as the tilt of the screen need to be considered in the lens design. If the trader tries to get away with one pair of glasses by using progressive lenses, he will always be looking for the small, gradated middle area or "sweet spot" of the lens to read his screen. This means that he will be moving his head awkwardly up and down, and side to side fatiguing his neck muscles. Wisely, Jack decides to go with the single level lens and goes to his office to measure his viewing distances.

Jack's ergonomic workstation is already set up. But, if you are experiencing eyestrain problems and are ready to experiment with ergonomic office adjustments, you might want to set up your office system again. Once you have established the crucial items – the level of the desk, the adequacy of the chair, the placement of the monitor, and the dynamic of the correct placement of fingers on the keyboard – test it for several days, if possible. When you are comfortable and satisfied with your position, have someone measure the distance between your eyes and your screen at least two or three times. If you are getting bifocals, you will also need to check the angle of the screen's tilt. Take these measurements to the ophthalmologist when you go to get your eyes checked. Plainly tell your doctor that you may need glasses for use at your computer as well as for reading and other close work

Lighting Your Office

Having already set up your ergonomic office, consider some lighting adjustments to benefit your eyes. Some specialists believe that improper lighting is the largest environmental factor contributing to visual discomfort. The Illuminating Engineering Society has established maximum luminance ratios that one might explore, but there are some simple lighting concepts to consider without calling in a lighting engineer. The best lighting situation is one where all visible objects in the field of view have equal brightness. In other words, the computer screen should not be much brighter than the wall behind it. Understand that office lighting also comes from windows and reflections from the surfaces in the room as well as from artificial light sources. You could have perfect ergonomic lighting with everything being a soft matte cream color and then place a large brass urn where it reflects light into your eyes or onto your screen and ruin the whole effort.

Beware of Glare

Glare is the stepchild of poor lighting. One glaring culprit is the common overhead fluorescent light fixture. Light leaves the fixture in a wide angle, resulting in light directly entering the trader's eyes. It is possible to direct this light downward by using louvers. A better solution is indirect lighting where the light is bounced off of the ceiling, resulting in a large, low luminance source of light for the room.

This information may seem sort of unnecessary to a trader who has been getting along well enough with his lighting. So, let's take a quick test for glare discomfort. Look at your screen and be aware of any bright lights in your peripheral vision. Then, shield your eyes with your hand, a baseball cap, or visor. Note whether you can sense an immediate improvement in your comfort level. Try this several times during different times of the day. If you notice an immediate improvement in comfort, imagine the cumulative effects of this glare for an entire day.

One way to create an immediate improvement in glare protection is to keep the visor on. Other ways include turning on one set of fluorescent lights, avoiding bright, reflective surfaces (office surfaces should be matte), and changing the brightness of the computer screen. You don't really want to screen off your window, especially if you have greenery in view, but outside light is usually the brightest and must be dealt with. Blinds will cut some of the light and if you are close by you can open them. Try to find a middle ground between ergonomic lighting and the calming effect of your view.

Improve Your Computer Display

Your computer display can contribute significantly to your eyestrain. You may be able to read a book for hours, but begin to feel eye irritation at the computer much sooner. This is because the text on the page is much crisper than the display on your computer screen. To prove this, simply print out a page of text on a laser printer and compare it with the same text on the screen. Although you will be unable to match the laser printer quality, there are several ways to improve the legibility of text on your screen. Good screen resolution is important, especially for extended work. The more pixels – the little dots from which characters can be formed – on the screen, the better. In case this isn't obvious, for more pixels, you'll need a better monitor. Black letters on a white background usually are best, but other combinations can be comfortable so long as the contrast between letters and background remains high.

Your text should be comfortably large. Experiment with text sizes and look for what makes your eyes relax but keeps you focused on the job at hand. Flicker beyond our ability to discern can also be causing visual difficulties. Use a monitor with higher refresh rates such as 70 Hz to relieve this problem. Adjust the screen contrast so that character definition and resolution is maximized. Finally, adjust the screen brightness to match the general brightness of the room. Even if you've never experienced eyestrain (yet!), make these adjustments to your display to optimize your general comfort at the screen.

Conclusion

Now, Jack has his glasses, which were measured and designed to work at the exact distance that he usually keeps his eyes from the screen. He sees the screen better and is able to work his last hour without eyestrain and its accompanying problems. Still, he plans to add louvers to his overhead fluorescent lighting to eliminate some glare that he discovered with our glare test. Currently, he is experimenting with variations on his computer display in an attempt to make the screen even more comfortable for his eyes. He has learned that he is able to focus on the job of trading with less stress when he can see the screen better and remain comfortable throughout his trading day.

SECTION 6
Handling the Worst Things

Chapter 25

MAKING THE BEST OF THE WORST EXPERIENCE

If you were faced with the worst experience that you could imagine, would you come through it stronger than before and ready to get back to your trading? Or would you emerge so badly bruised that your scars would effectively seal you off from future success?

As a trader, you constantly risk facing bad situations, whether it is in your professional or in your personal life. The market is clearly not a benevolent force and, whether you are a trader or not, you face the potential for pain in your personal life. The question is "Are you prepared?"

When the worst happens, it is likely that you will feel helpless and powerless at first. Nevertheless, you have two choices that are always within your control, even if you may not be aware of them.

First, you can choose how you feel about the experience. This is true although you may find yourself resisting the idea. Most people believe that they have no choice about how they feel. To paraphrase Warner Earhardt, the EST guru, you may not get to choose what you experience, but you can choose how you experience it. For example, you cannot choose whether or not to be involved in a market crash, but you can choose to experience it as a tragedy or as an opportunity, such as a major lesson learned.

Second, you can choose to act as if you feel a particular way. "Acting as if" is a choice. In the midst of a crisis, some people who are filled with fear will act as if they are calm and know exactly what to do. This set of actions requires a choice. The results, of course, are counter to logic. The frightened individual who is acting as if he is fearless begins to feel in control and those people who are around him believe that he is in control. They calm down and the crisis becomes more manageable.

The Things You Know

The first step in making the best of the worst experiences is to take stock of what you already know. I strongly believe in assessing your resources, regardless of the problem. One of your most important resources is what you know about a situation, even before it develops.

By now, the first thing you should know is that to be human is to be in the way of things that happen. No one gets out of this life without experiencing pain, loss, catastrophe, illness, betrayal, disappointment, humiliation, rejection, and heartache to some extent. The list of possible personal and professional losses is long and distinguished. Those of us who realize and accept this fact are in a much better position, not only to lessen the pain, but to shorten the list.

Knowing in advance that good and bad "things" are going to happen in life allows you to plan for them. One of the most important steps in creating a successful life for a trader is to take the time to plan. This plan includes not only a business plan, but a plan for all the other areas of your life. I call this comprehensive plan a life plan, which includes an assessment of your resources and contingency planning. Contingency planning assumes that major things are going to happen that are either wonderful or terrible, or possibly both. So, you need a plan for all of the things that can go wrong as well as all the things that can go right. My book, _Getting More Out of Life_, contains a life plan that has made a big difference for people by getting them to focus on the positive things in their lives while preparing for the things that can go wrong. While you do not need my book to do this, you need a form of this type for planning in order to be prepared for life.

We are usually pretty clear on the negative impact when things go wrong. Unfortunately, most people are totally unprepared for all of the things that can go wrong as the result of things going right. When people realize their wildest dreams and make that fortune, acquire that mansion, or win that lottery, they have seldom planned for the isolation, the loss of self-confidence, the paranoia, the ennui, or the stress that can result from becoming wildly successful.

The second thing you should know is how you will react to events in your life, as well as how the people around you, who have a direct influence on your life, will behave. To have an understanding, beforehand, of how you and your significant people will react is like going into battle, knowing the enemy's plans.

For example, if you have just experienced a major loss in the markets, do you know how you will react? How will your wife, partners, and investors react? Let's say that you already know that your first reaction will be to go into a state of denial, your wife will get hysterical and threaten to leave, your partner will hit the first bar to anesthetize the pain, and your investors will threaten to sue. Although this is all bad news, the fact that you know in advance how everyone will react will allow you much needed time to develop your game plan. Now you have a chance to create a response to all of these reactions. Suppose, however, that you know in advance that you can rely on the significant people around you to be supportive, philosophical, and prepared to take action to correct the problem immediately. This information is also incredibly helpful.

Bill Clinton, regardless of your political leanings, has a very predictable and successful way of responding to a crisis. From observation and accounts of the people closest to him, he compartmentalizes his life so that he puts the crisis in one box while attending to everything else. As a consummate politician, he finds someone to take the fall for the crisis, preferably someone who has pledged loyalty to him. Then, he recreates the truth so that it best fits his needs. This reconstruction of the truth and his appearance of confidence allow the people who believe in him to continue to believe in him. And best of all, he continues to believe in himself. In this manner, he rides out one crisis after another. If you are dependent upon him in a crisis you know how he will react, which is very important information.

Now that you know how you are going to respond and how the significant others in your life will react, factor this information into your contingency plans. As an example, if the region where you live is prone to floods or hurricanes and you need to plan for this contingency, can you count on your state's governor to send out the National Guard immediately to help or will you be on your own for a long time? What can you count on and what can you not count on? To what extent will you personally go to work things out and to what extent will others have to?

Planning in Advance

Taking this process one step further means that you should also look past the important people in your life. As a trader, you need to be looking to the industries and networks of services upon which you rely for their own predictable reactions to crisis or challenge. How reliable are they under stress? When the price of oil reached astronomical heights, were you prepared? Can you count on OPEC to keep your best interests at heart? What about their past track record for taking sound actions?

Let's take an example in your daily trading. Suppose you have taken a trade and the bottom drops out of the market. Suddenly, the cable goes out. What contingencies do you have in place? Even if the situation is extremely difficult, you need to move with confidence. That confidence will come with careful planning.

Losing Opportunity

In observing your own patterns of behavior, do you know what sets you off and makes you angry, anxious, worried, defeated, miserable, or frightened? Did anything happen today to make you feel that way? Search for the triggers to those deep-seated, negative feelings so that you know what you can expect to create them. It is not a question of whether or not these feelings are valid, because all feelings are valid. The important thing is that you know that you are eventually going to get over these feelings and the situation that triggered them. Look back, imagine the time you spent being angry, anxious, or miserable more than you needed to feel and realize the amount of time you wasted and the lost opportunities.

Why is it important to put the negative feelings aside as soon as possible? Let's suppose that you have taken a big loss in the markets. Afterwards, you spent a great deal of time feeling angry, upset, fearful, and distraught. Will you be able to see the major opportunity for a winning trade that is following the loss? Will you be able to capitalize on that opportunity if you are unable to see it because you are consumed with feelings of inadequacy due to the previous loss? The undue attachment to negative feelings usually comes at a great price. This price can also occur in your personal life. If you are still suffering over a loss in the markets or a rejection in your personal life, you may miss out on a wonderful relationship that is available to you at this moment. Most opportunities have a very brief shelf life, especially relationship and market opportunities.

Exercise

If you do not work on your life planning with contingencies, negative experiences will most likely result in prolonged negative emotional reactions. To abbreviate the duration of these reactions, follow these steps:

1. First, you have to acknowledge to yourself the emotions you are feeling and the story that you have created about the experience.
2. As you acknowledge the story you have created for yourself, pull back from it and go to the big picture.
3. As you observe the situation that is creating the negative emotions from the greatest distance you can give it, ask yourself, "How long do I really want to be in this state?"
4. As you ask yourself this question, focus your attention on the part of your abdomen where your navel is and take three deep, long breaths.
5. Center yourself by placing your focus on your middle and see a brilliant light going through you. Maintain your focus on your navel area.
6. Now, use this highly empowering phrase: "We can do this!"

This phrase, "We can do this!" means that whatever the challenge, you will be able to overcome it and that you will not be doing it alone. You are acknowledging the fact that you are not all-powerful and omnipotent. However, with the aid of the Universal Power, you will be able to prevail. You are recognizing the fact that, with God, all is possible. It is not important that you believe in God to tap into the power of this resource. You are giving a message to your neurological system that it needs to be directed in a powerful way to succeed.

Once you center yourself and utter this phrase, you are well on your way to limiting the damage that will occur in the worst situations and becoming a successful survivor. Empowered with this message to your neurology, you will find yourself being able to think creatively and take the kind of audacious actions that many crises require for a successful outcome. I have often found that successful survivors had already considered the possibility of a similar crisis or set of circumstances occurring. As a result, they had a rough idea of how they would react and what they could possibly do to survive.

For example, one of my most successful clients is a trader whose family had to escape from a totalitarian political system. This young son was primed to handle all of the crises and catastrophes that he encountered later on in his trading as a result of all of the planning and courage that was required for his family's successful escape. He understands planning, danger, and risk. But most of all, he understands the power of believing in the outcome.

Conclusion

In the midst of the worst possible circumstance, most people are angered and frustrated by the statement that there is opportunity behind every bad situation. Even if that is true, the unprepared get stuck in their reactions and negative feelings so that they cannot see or capitalize on the possibilities.

Regardless of what happens, it is possible to abbreviate the duration of the power draining emotions and thoughts to seize the opportunities hidden behind a catastrophe. The first step to making the best of the worst experience is to plan for its occurrence. The second step is to arm yourself with the best possible psychological defense against emotional paralysis by using the exercise outlined above. A life plan that includes your resources, what you know, and your contingency responses is like going into battle with superior weaponry. Your chances of emerging unscathed and victorious are improved immeasurably and you will have made the best of the worst that can happen.

Chapter 26

_____

CHANGE

Rapid Changes Everywhere

The world is undergoing technological change at a rate that is unprecedented in the history of mankind. Since the beginning of the Industrial Revolution, change has been snowballing through the rapid advances in innovation. Today, you can buy the newest, neatest computer representing a substantial monetary investment. Tomorrow, it becomes an obsolete doorstop as newer, faster designs roll from the assembly line. As a floor trader, you have invested a lifetime of savings to purchase a seat on an exchange that will ensure your financial security for the rest of your life. Suddenly, your $500,000 investment is a rapidly diminishing asset as a result of change. Along this same line of thought, the old adage that land is the most solid investment is no longer valid in parts of the country where the government can seize your land or where property values can instantly plummet because of change.

Major Market Changes

For traders, major changes are afoot. We are currently facing the potential for a major downturn in the markets after years of unprecedented expansion. There is an entire generation of investors who have never experienced a bear market. Recently, I overheard a verbal exchange between a young woman who was an electronic day trader and a salesman who ran a booth at an investor convention. In presenting the capabilities of his new software, the salesman said, "Here is where the software would give you the signal to 'go long' and here is the place where you would 'go short.'" The young woman stopped him in mid-sentence. "I've heard that phrase before! What does 'go short' mean?"

Change to Electronic Trading

We are facing the eventual closure of the exchanges as they have operated for decades with the transition to electronic trading. The sounds of the 'Old World' outcry of traders announcing their commodity trades could soon be gone forever as we speed on to this next level of trading. Because of the exploding changes due to these technological innovations, we are constantly bombarded with having to deal with the issues brought about by change. As traders, we work so hard to develop our technology and systems only to find that they often no longer apply to the current markets.

Change Upsets the Balance in a Trader's Life.

Not only does a trader have to deal with the changes in his professional life, he also has to deal with the changes in his private life. In order to perform successfully, a trader has to manage all of the changes that occur in his life on a daily basis because they affect his trading decisions. Regardless of how well a trader deals with these changes or whether the changes are good or bad, any change can upset a trader's balance. For example, a family is a working unit to which each member contributes an essential part of the unit's energy. If one family member leaves or changes his contribution, the whole unit is affected. For that reason, a change in a family member can be an unexpected source of change in a trader's life. Recently, the wife of one of my clients lost her mother. Since her mother's death, the trader's wife has been out of balance. Her imbalance has created an imbalance in her husband that has affected his trading.

Other Examples:
- When a child goes off to college, he stops contributing his efforts to keeping up the household. In addition to the loss of his contribution, his education consumes family resources or his absence suddenly increases leisure time. While some changes seem positive, every change causes imbalance.
- If a child returns home to live, his presence can create an additional drain on resources even though he may be attempting to contribute to the family.
- If a family member becomes ill – not only does the illness create a loss in that member's contribution to the family but it can also suddenly and rapidly consume family energy and resources.

Each change requires a major readjustment in the entire family unit. Sometimes the net change is small and there is no discernable difference in the resources consumed. However, the emotional toll in making the necessary adjustments is much more difficult to determine. In all of these examples, a physical and economic consequence exists that can increase the pressure on a trader putting him out of balance so that his trading is affected.

You might not associate these changes with problems in your trading. But, it is important to notice the changes in your environment because awareness helps you act appropriately in making decisions about trading and risk during times of dislocation. In addition to the obvious day-to-day personal changes that occur in a trader's life, major social and physical forces are at work that carry long-term ramifications for a trader. For example:

1. Aging and Expanded Life Expectancy

The human life span has more than doubled since the days of Romeo and Juliet, the two lovers barely in their teens. In Elizabethan times, the average man lived to age 30 or 35. With an expanded life expectancy, we face problems associated with maturing and aging that were not even known to our ancestors. We must plan for our old age when in centuries past no one actually reached it.

The good news for traders is that as their life span increases, their trading careers are also lengthened. The result is a double-edged sword: the opportunity to grow into other areas of trading and the problem of what to do when you are tired of trading and want to move on to other things.

2. Family Structure

The breakdown of the extended family began as soon as people began to leave the communities where they were raised for educational and economic opportunities and political freedom. The ease of modern transportation has sent us to every corner of the world. But, the nuclear family has undergone rapid disintegration. Marriage is considered an obsolete institution in many circles. For those who do get married, the promise of life-long commitment does not seem to last as long as even the brief Elizabethan life span would have suggested.

What does this imply for traders? As a profession, traders face the prospect of divorce at higher than the national average due to the stress of their jobs on their families. Divorce is a major life change that has a great implication for a trader's career and can sidetrack trading success for a significant period of time.

3. Religion

In the latter half of the Twentieth Century, attendance at traditional churches and synagogues has seen a steady decline. Now, the trend seems to be reversing. Baby Boomers born in the Forties and Fifties are coming of age spiritually. They appreciate the tradition of the old churches, but they are demanding changes in the requirement to adhere to a dogma they find irrational and outdated. Furthermore, having been raised on the feeling of personal empowerment, these mid-lifers feel less reason to adhere to the teachings of the church based on church authority.

Until recently, many traders had lost a sense of the importance of religion in their lives. However, many are now discovering the new spiritual movements and finding that a spiritual life enhances their personal and professional lives. In addition, many traders have found that their new spiritual practices and understandings have given new life to their older, traditional religious practices.

4. Dealing with Change

How do you deal with these changes in a way that is the most effective for you requiring the least amount of time, wear and tear, and dislocation? The first step, which is also the best step, is to prepare for change. Make change part of your contingency planning for your life and for your business. In that way, you will know what to do when change occurs. This is the pro-active approach to change.

But, what should you do if you have not taken the time to create a plan?

5. Recognizing that a Change has Occurred

There will be an upset in the balance of your life that will most likely affect your trading.

6. Making a Decision About how You Want to Handle the Change

Once you recognize the change and accept the fact that this change will affect your trading, the most obvious answer is "I want to handle it immediately, so that it won't affect my trading." Unfortunately, when you are in the muck of change, you will tend to push aside the reality of the change or plunge through it as though it does not exist. Knowing in advance that you will try to avoid dealing with change and having a strategy for coping will help you to stay more focused.

7. Interpreting the Change Positively

Take a piece of paper and draw a line down the middle. On one side, list all of the negative ways the change will affect you and on the other side, list all of the positive ways the change will affect you.

Example: Suppose you have made a terrific living trading on the floor. You have not developed a methodology or system, but trade intuitively. You do not have a lot of education in math and technology. Suddenly, you are facing the loss of your floor-trading career and you will be sitting behind a desk with no background in technical trading.

Negative interpretations: Because you will have to master many challenges and deal with considerable change, you will:

- Not be making the same amount of money at first. You will have to be prepared for some economic dislocation. The consequences could be serious, requiring you to sell your house and move to smaller and more austere accommodations. You could fail to get off to a good start, damaging your confidence and affecting your ability to trade and having to go into an entirely different field if you do not do well.
- Have to learn to use a great deal of new and technical information
- Be required to master a computer, which you have never used before
- Be working alone and no longer part of the camaraderie of the floor
- Have to set up your own workstation
- Not be able to trade intuitively, as you have done in the past

Positive interpretations: Although it is likely that you may start off not making the same amount of money as before, it is clear that there are off-the-floor traders who make a great deal of money. You can be one of them. In addition, you may:

- Take a lot of pressure off of yourself and discover new resources in yourself and your environment as a result of having to downscale
- Gain important new skills by learning how to use a computer to trade, making you more competitive, not only in your profession, but in new fields, as well. These new skills can also increase your sense of competence, thereby increasing your self-confidence.
- Set up shop with another trader or group of traders
- Work alone, but you are not required to do so
- Set up an office from home and stop commuting into the city, a change that is viewed as a great side benefit by many electronic traders
- Dramatically improve your health as you spend less time on your feet, less time wearing out your back, your ears, your voice, and your adrenal glands
- Eventually trade intuitively, using your years of experience in developing your intuitive skills

8. **While in the Transition Stage of Change, Stop Trading, Lighten up on Trading, or Adjust Your Risk to Minimize Losses.**

9. **During this Period, Realize that You are Emotionally and Physically out of Balance.**
   Focus on rejuvenating this part of your life before you get back into the full swing of your trading.

Conclusion

Change means imbalance for a trader, regardless of its source or whether it is a good or bad change. This imbalance affects trading performance. Therefore, a trader who wants to maintain a steady and successful career must plan for change and maintain a strategy for dealing with it. It is impossible to avoid change, but it is possible to minimize the damage it can do professionally and personally.

Chapter 27

_____

FACING CONFLICT

Making money in the markets eventually requires that you cope with changes or problems involving conflict. If you can face the issues and handle the conflict well, you get to move on to the next step in your quest for success. If you fail at the challenge, you are required to go back a step.

Recently, I worked with a group of investment brokers who were reeling from the steep downward spiral in the markets. Nearly all of these highly successful men and women had clients who had lost a substantial portion of their wealth almost overnight. Since some of these brokers were young and had never been through a bear market before, this was a terrible shock to them.

How did they respond? The group appeared to divide into two common, distinct, and completely opposite reactions.

The Reactive Strategy

The first response was to avoid all contact with their clients. In other words, go into hiding. Clearly, these brokers were responding to fear. It takes bravery to willingly face the prospect of a screaming, crying, or angry voice on the other end of the telephone. Suppose the client accused you of being responsible for putting him into an investment package that resulted in the loss of everything he had? What would your response be?

The Proactive Strategy

The other response was to be proactive and call the clients before they called you. This strategy allowed the broker to hold the clients' hands and assure them that they were there for them. Done early in the game, this proactive response cuts off hysteria and blame at the pass, while keeping the lines of communication open for the future. Many of the most seasoned brokers were able to employ this strategy. They had already heard the worst from their clients. Of course, there were some of the older brokers who were too shell-shocked from earlier times to try this strategy. These brokers were like men who had gone into a protracted battle and fallen apart afterwards at the sound of a car backfiring.

The New Fashion Strategy

A company that specializes in communications software proposed a third strategy to this group. A recorded message that sounds like the unrecorded voice of the broker is placed on the client's machine when the phone is not picked up. Thus, the broker is able to send a proactive message of support without having to encounter the possibility of an emotional scene or attack.

Now, if you were a client, which one of these responses would you prefer from your broker? Truthfully, some clients would prefer to have the opportunity to vent a considerable amount of rage on their broker. But, once the anger has been vented, would you not want to have a broker who was willing to hold your hand and help you to put together a strategy for coping with a bad situation?

Other Avoided Conflicts

Whether you are a broker or trader, there are various types of conflict that you need to make choices on how to approach:

- A trader has lost more money than he can afford to lose. He is afraid to tell his wife, so he becomes distant. She misinterprets his reaction, taking it personally, and begins to distance herself, as well. The marriage falls apart while the business is crumbling.

- A trader has a business partner whose style of trading, habits, level of commitment to the business, or business practices becomes a source of concern. Rather than talk to his partner, the trader fears conflict and says nothing. The situation deteriorates so that the partnership dies, along with the business.

Are you avoiding the proactive choice of dealing with a conflict? Perhaps, you should consider the long-range consequences of conflict avoidance. It is probably not your best choice.

Chapter 28

_____

FAILING YOUR WAY TO SUCCESS

Would you choose to do the most difficult things in the most difficult ways, while failing at every step in order to succeed?

Now, before you say, "No, why in the world would I do that?" I want you to realize that most people who become professional traders make the choice to fail their way to success. Of course, they do not make this choice knowingly, but the end result of their decisions is to take this path.

It is generally understood that the way to succeed in professions other than trading requires advanced education and degrees, plus years of training and personal development. This is not so with trading. Unfortunately, people can enter the profession of trading without this type of preparation, but they cannot succeed over time without it.

Doing it all Wrong

Several years ago, I conducted a phone consultation with a young trader named Phil. With his trust fund in hand, a knack for getting top grades without having to work hard, and a love of excitement, Phil had decided to enter the world of trading and make a killing in the markets. After all, he had read about all of the money that top traders were making. With his advantages and high intelligence, he assumed that he would be successful in a short time.

Unfortunately, during that short time, he had his first loss proving that the markets were not fair. Still, he had expected a few losses, so, he continued to trade without any hard preparation and he continued to lose. As the losses mounted and became more serious, he began to suffer the usual emotional reactions to loss: fear, insecurity, hesitancy, and inconsistency. Since Phil had not spent years in developing a system, he was lost at sea as to what he was doing and why. Instead of being easy, trading had become difficult, arcane, and painful.

Phil decided to get coaching without paying for the service and called me to see if I could fix the problem. When queried about his preparation for trading, Phil brushed off the subject lightly, as though it had little relevance to his situation. Months later, he called again and was willing to listen but still unwilling to take the right action. Since Phil had never had to work hard before, he was dismayed at the level of commitment that successful trading would require of him. Not only would he need to study the markets, read everything in sight, attend seminars, and develop and test a working system, he would also have to work on his psychology. Phil was listening but once again, he was listening between the lines to see how he could beat the system. Here are some of the steps he took on the easy way to failing at trading:

1. **The Hot Tip**

   Phil did not want to put in the required time and effort while developing his own system. Instead, he used his brainpower to come up with what he thought was an excellent idea. Why not find someone who would provide him with the right information? He started frequenting the local watering holes where traders went after hours. He became the acquaintance of several traders, found out which trader was generally regarded as the best of the lot, and focused his attention on him. The trader that Phil selected was named Jim and soon, Jim was feeding Phil hot tips over beer and pretzel sticks. This system worked very well for three months. Then, while using one of Jim's tips, Phil lost a significant amount of money. Feeling bruised, shaken, and betrayed, Phil waited for Jim at the watering hole that night to find out what had happened. To his dismay, he discovered that Jim had escaped with only a minor scrape. As Phil pressed to find out why he had lost and Jim had not, Phil crossed the line of their friendship. An angry Jim told him to do his own homework and stop using him. It was the end of their friendship and the end of Phil's free hot tips.

2. **The Magic Guru**

   Then, Phil decided that he would resort to his old, standby strategy: if he could not get success for free, he would pay for it. He started with a trip to the local book warehouse that had a wall of books on every subject. As he looked through the books, he found a famous book on trading by a guru whose name even Phil had heard. For the first time, Phil was seriously reading and learning about trading. In his excitement and newfound passion for trading, this book became Phil's bible. He learned everything he could from the book and came to the point of breaking even. Unfortunately, over time, he began to see that the book had failed him at certain points and that he was not able to put into practice all that the book instructed him to do. Once again, he lost heavily.

   At this point, Phil thought that perhaps he needed more current advice. Checking around, he found a newsletter that was regarded as the best one around. It provided weekly advice and strategies, market updates, and current research. This expensive newsletter was highly sophisticated and technical; in fact, it was too much for Phil to comprehend with his limited exposure to the math and concepts involved. To utilize the valuable information from this service, he would have to devote himself to studying technical trading and the challenging math that underpins it. Although Phil had done reasonably well at math in school, he had no interest in submitting again to its demands.

3. The Magic System

Phil resorted to paying for success once again. He decided that he needed to buy a proven system. To his credit, Phil did some fairly extensive research and purchased one of the most expensive and best-regarded systems available. What Phil wanted was a mechanical system that anyone could follow. The problem was that Phil was not just anyone and when it came down to following the rules of the system even when he thought he saw a loss or an opportunity developing, he could not follow the system. Soon, he was breaking every rule of the system and ignoring all of the signals. The result: heavy drawdowns.

It was at this point that Phil called again. Over a year and a half had passed since I had heard from him, and he was sounding less confident of himself. In fact, he was getting ready to leave trading if this last round of strategies did not pay off.

4. The Magic Therapy

When everything else failed, Phil decided to come to a *Trading on Target Seminar*, still without commitment on his mind. He was once again attempting to find an outside source to solve his basic trading problems. What he found at the seminar from listening to the other attendees and the material presented was that all along, he was trying to take a short-cut while only making his path longer. He decided on private consultation. When I took Phil on as a client, it was before I had the rule that a trader had to have a system or methodology that he believed would work. The only thing between Phil and his success was his own psychological sabotage.

As we began to look at Phil's personal strategies, attitudes, and beliefs, it became clear that he had stacked the deck against himself. His patterns of behavior were filled with a daily regime of self-destructive acts. He abused his health by living on junk food, getting too little exercise and sleep, and consuming too much alcohol and drugs. When he was not engaged in trading, he filled his spare time with long hours on the couch watching television or cruising the local clubs with friends attempting to pick up women. He belonged to no organizations, churches, or clubs. He had no family and no strong friendships to support him.

All of Phil's life choices were based on a set of beliefs and attitudes that were anathema to success. He believed that life was a game where you simply found the fastest and easiest strategy to win. Having won easily in every game he had played as a young man, Phil was accustomed to winning and came to believe that he deserved to win by virtue of his natural superiority. If he found that he was losing, he did not hesitate to cheat or stack the deck in his favor since it was clearly unfair for him to lose. Once he had experienced losses in the markets, he was angered and wanted revenge. Phil knew now that if he were to succeed, he would have to go back to square one and start with a plan.

Dedicated Losers

Phil's trading odyssey is by no means a unique one. Many traders employ similar strategies. If they perceive trading as a game, and not as a profession, they will attempt to play at it as opposed to working at it. Once a trader has established a mental picture of "how things are," he will unconsciously look for evidence that supports his picture of reality or create circumstances that reinforce that picture.

If a trader has established a pattern of failing his way to success as the way to approach trading, he will be unable to see that his approach is wrong. He may work harder to show himself that he is on the right track rather than admit that he may be wrong. I have seen traders who were deeply committed to a self-destructive, failing strategy do extremely well over the short term because they put so much energy into their approach that it created its own wake. Eventually, however, like a soufflé that expands on air, the system will collapse on itself, blowing the trader right off of the field.

More of these failing strategies are:

1. **Trading is a game, so I'll play it like one**.
   This was one of Phil's losing beliefs. Trading is a serious profession that makes its money from people who don't see it as one.

2. **Trading provides on-the-job training, so I don't need to go into it completely prepared**.
   By the time you have learned the important lessons from the on-the-job training, you are out of the business.

3. **I can leverage a small amount of capital into a fortune, so I don't need to be well capitalized**.
   Under capitalization is the single most common reason for a trader to wash out early in the game. Far too many new traders start out with $5,000 nest eggs that are rapidly consumed by the vultures.

4. **I can buy my way to success**.
   Phil was actually a piker in this game compared to some of the super-financed traders I have met. If too many traders go into trading under-capitalized, there are also a number of traders who are over-capitalized. They spend small fortunes attempting to buy success. Yes, it is important to have solid capital behind you, but money cannot replace commitment, research, mastery, self-discipline, emotional mastery, and time.

5. **I do not need to practice self-discipline in my money management or in my life because I have brilliance and/or a great system and/or unlimited resources**.
   The term "self-discipline" conjures up images of pain, loss, or sacrifice to many people who are unable or unwilling to deal with those feelings. People who have not practiced self-discipline in their former lives will not come by it easily in their trading lives. But, no trader succeeds over time without a great deal of self-discipline.

6. **I can borrow the money and pay it back in no time.**

Traders who borrow the money from their children's college funds, in-laws, friends, or from home equity are trading with the same odds as playing roulette in Las Vegas, because they are working with "scared money." When in a draw down, visualizations of loved ones losing the benefit of money accumulated for their future needs will keep you in a drawdown state of mind, where sabotage is king.

7. **I can trade from anyplace.**

Trading in an environment that is not conducive to trading is another shortcut that is a sure way of failing to succeed. A trader's home may have a secure and comfortable room that is completely separate from any of the demands of the home and still not allow a trader to trade from home. For example, when his trading is not going well, the temptation to visit the TV room or the kitchen or play with the children can be overwhelming. These temptations can be overwhelming even if things are not going badly. In the meantime, the rest of the world will not honor your working time if you are even a tiny bit available to interruptions.

8. **I don't need to test my system. I know it works.**

The time required to adequately test a system seems like a waste of time for a trader who has already invested a great deal of time developing it. By the time a trader has finally completed his research and developed his system, he is likely to believe it is infallible or at least a winning system. The only problem is that his unconscious knows the difference. Conflict will arise as a result, and make it difficult to take action.

9. **This psychology business is nonsense.**

I'm fine. This may be one of the most common failing strategies. After spending years creating the capital necessary to trade, doing research and developing and testing a system, the average committed trader is often not interested in looking within himself for the answers to his future success. This response is especially true with mechanical traders who assume that they will respond like machines when their system gives them a trading signal. I have sat in trading rooms with traders who believed this to be true and watched them quietly convulsing inside. Unfortunately, we are still human and we are wired in our brains to react emotionally to stimuli. These reactions have evolved over millions of years in order to protect us. We will do what is necessary to protect ourselves from the pain of loss, only to create more loss in the process.

10. **My goal is simple: Make a lot of money.**

What is wrong with this strategy? It's only a part of the answer. Yes, a trader needs to go into trading with the idea of making money. But, he needs to have a good relationship with money in the past in order to have a good one in the future. In addition, it cannot be the only goal, because a trader must enjoy the process of trading or he will create a lot of exciting and interesting ways to lose money.

How to Get Off the Failing Path

It is impossible to change the direction of a diesel train, loaded with 75 cars of cargo, plunging down the tracks at ninety miles an hour. However, it only takes one broken rail pin to derail the train and destroy the entire shipment. Turning a trader to a constructive, success path that will lead to long-term success after he has been on a misguided path without transformation of perception is equally impossible. But, destroying his trading career can be as easy as derailing that train. Like they tell new and frightened attendees at their first AA meeting, the first step to success is admitting that you have a problem and that you need help. Taking that first step for traders often comes only after a series of painful losses or maybe not at all.

Instead of waiting for your career to be permanently derailed, I have a few suggestions that can help you switch tracks without crashing. The first and most important step is for you to re-evaluate your business plan. What? You have none? Well, that does not surprise me. Traders who have completed a comprehensive business plan are, by definition, on the right track. But, they are in the great minority. A good business plan for trading requires you to confront all of the issues discussed in this article and many more.

A good business plan for trading requires you to approach trading as the business that it is. You have to understand your goals and develop the constructive strategy that will allow you to reach them. For example, you will have to establish the right trading environment, develop the right kind of capital and personal resources, work on your self-discipline and examine your psychology to make certain that it will support your goals. A good business plan must be followed, periodically updated and reviewed. It will require you to associate with people who are trained in business practices, such as accountants, bankers, lawyers, and suppliers of services. And it will require you to create achievable goals along the way with timetables for completion.

A good business plan will be able to show you if you are in trouble and need help. Then, you will have a reason to call for help and a means of measuring your progress. A good business plan will prepare you for every contingency so that you will know every action to take.

Oh, by the way, after I got Phil to work on his trading business plan, he had a trading epiphany. He suddenly got it! Trading was a business and a profession all wrapped up in one. It wasn't a game any more and Phil made the commitment to do what it took to succeed. Funny thing, by following his plan, life and trading became a lot easier than working to take the easy path of failing his way to success. All of this was several years ago and Phil now is a well-established trader. He's married with a second child on the way.

Conclusion

Failing your way to success is a common, but painful way to travel, especially when traders reach the dead end at full speed. Often, the most immediately successful trading strategies are losing strategies over time. For traders who have not made the full commitment to trading as a profession and have not done the planning required for long-term success, the choices will make sense at the time. They will look easy, simple, and quick, but they will seldom be the right ones. The way off of this path is doing what you should have done in the very beginning: take the time to create a complete trading business plan and succeed your way to success, instead.

Chapter 29

TRADER SUICIDE

Recently, a trader called me in a panic. His brother was in the hospital after having taken an overdose of sleeping pills to end his life. My client, Joe, felt helpless in the situation because he did not know how to handle the problem nor did he know what words to say to his brother.

"How," Joe asked me, "does someone get to the point of choosing suicide as the only option?"

This has become a very important question for traders. Over the past decade, I have heard far too many traders say that they wanted to end their lives. Fortunately, I was able to help them find a way out of their desperation so that none of them actually took their own life. For a trader, there are many ways to commit suicide besides taking his life. A trader can:

- Destroy his career and lose everything he has in one glorious act of self-immolation. Countless traders have sat transfixed before their computers as they watched their entire trading capital base evaporate before their eyes in a single trade.

- Do it the slow way, by sabotaging his trading so that he loses his way to a trading death. The easiest and most common way for a trader to do this is by failing to follow his rules or methodology.

- Destroy the supports around him - his spouse, family, and friends - so that he must face his world alone and unloved. Many traders fail to attend to their personal lives by neglecting or mistreating their wives, children, and the people who have consistently cared about them. It is common for these traders to ignore clear signs of trouble ahead and continue to destroy these relationships.

- Engage in self-destructive behaviors that ensure a trading death or a physical downfall. For example, a trader can commit acts of fraud or illegal financial dealings that would end his career. Or, he can drink excessively, take drugs, and generally abuse himself physically so that he can no longer trade.

A Final Solution to a Temporary Problem

What would bring a trader to the point of literal or metaphorical suicide? Let us take a look at some of the most common causes:

1. **Cracking the Nut**
   The life of a successful trader eventually fills up with expensive toys, a beautiful home, and the other trappings of affluence. After a while, the successful trader begins to define his life and his self-worth by these material expressions of his success. For most traders, the result of affluence is a set of built-in expenses that become the trader's monthly nut to crack. The more successful a trader is and the longer he has been successful, the bigger the nut he must crack each month. For example, he might have payments on a second home, private school for the kids, maintenance of the pool and grounds, housekeeping staff, country club dues, and other social obligations.

   What happens to this successful trader, if he should experience a major loss or a set of losses that threatens to take all of these trappings away? Suddenly, he is consumed with fear and a sense of despair. How can he continue to crack that enormous nut next month and the next? How will he pay the mortgage? Will he have to take his daughter out of the expensive college she is attending? And what will happen to his wife if she suddenly has to withdraw from the country club? How will he tell his family that their lives are suddenly going to change and how will he be able to face his relatives, his neighbors, and his trader friends?

   Confronted with the loss of face, with the loss of his social prestige and standing, with the emotional turmoil of his family, and the loss of his good credit and financial security, the successful trader can succumb to panic and despair. He sees no way out. The nut is too large to crack and he sees no way to do it other than what he has always done in the past. His thinking has become so inflexible that he has lost his ability to problem-solve out of the box that he has built for himself. At this point, suicide can begin to look like the only option left to him. Here is where the chorus sings the refrain: "Suicide is the only option."

2. **The Threat of Change**
   Once again, it is the long-term, successful trader who is most likely to feel trapped, without options, when he is confronted by change. This is especially true if the change relates to the way he makes his livelihood. In recent times, as floor traders have been forced from the floor into electronic trading, many of them have experienced a sense of personal despair, convinced that they cannot make the transition. As the displaced trader watches his teenage son perform miracles on his

laptop computer, this trader with a high school education does not even know how to turn a computer on. He has not read a technical book since high school. The thought of having to learn a technology so foreign to his experience is too threatening to consider. Topping that is the fear of failure and embarrassment. He, too, begins to contemplate the loss of his material trappings. Overwhelmed with a sense that he is facing an impossible situation, this trader may decide…Refrain Second Verse.

3. **The Perfect System that Failed**

A sense of despair that has no cure can overcome the trader who has been a successful technical trader for a long time and suddenly discovers that his predictable and highly profitable system begins to fail. After years of research and testing, he had made that system work so well that it has generated a substantial and reliable income. But, the market changed and his system no longer works. For a trader who has put years into his system, he may no longer know how or be willing to go back to square one and do it all over again. In creating that perfect system, the trader created a lifestyle and he feels incapable of retreating back to square one. He does not want to go back to the learning phase again. Like the other traders who contemplate ending their lives, he was unprepared for what could go wrong. He thought that his life as he knew it would always be there. Refrain Third Verse.

4. **Emotional Snowballing**

When traders are overloaded with emotional turmoil, they are less likely to see other options that are available to them. As emotional turmoil builds, so does the level of pain it creates. Along with that pain comes an increase in the level of background noise in our consciousness that prevents us from hearing the voices of reason and creative problem solving in our brain. As a result, the only thing we can see is escape. That escape usually comes from the fact that we do not want to feel the pain that we created in ourselves.

Usually, there is a particular event that starts the snowballing to end one's life or one's trading life. However, sometimes a series of small steps over a period of time will lead to that one last step that makes a trader feel so overloaded with emotional turmoil that he must do whatever it takes to stop the pain.

What are some of those events that can start the emotional snowballing? Trading losses are clearly some of the most powerful causes. Even a long-term trader can succumb to emotional snowballing from a loss that he was not expecting. But, personal losses and conflicts can create emotional snowballing just as effectively. Traders who are going through marital conflicts, separation, and divorce can be torn by emotions. A death or illness in the family or having been in an accident or natural disaster can all begin the process of emotional snowballing. Refrain Fourth Verse.

Prevention is the Best Cure

- The very best way to deal with the problem of trader suicide is to put into place the steps that would prevent you from reaching that stage in your life.

- Recognize the fact that you are putting yourself in a position to emotionally snowball by learning to take your own emotional temperature. You can do this by listening to how you are talking to yourself and your level of optimism.

- Do not overload yourself with too many responsibilities or time and financial obligations.

- Learn to recognize when you are putting yourself in a situation that has potential for collapse. If you see a situation brewing, nip it in the bud.

- When you have taken all of the precautions that you can to protect yourself by planning for all the things that could go wrong, recognize the fact that you cannot predict all the circumstances around you and develop a plan B.

- Take care of yourself physically and emotionally. Give yourself room to make mistakes and time to heal from those mistakes.

- Support the relationships in your life. Attend to them the way you do your trading.

- Some people are very loyal to the institutions for which they work and feel secure in their positions while failing to see that the institution itself may not be secure. For that reason, it is important to be constantly building bridges from your job into another institution or position.

- Learn to identify your skills and experience so that you can transfer them to another position. It is important to be prepared for the fact that you may not be able to earn the same amount of money that you did previously and that you might have to deal with age prejudice.

Conclusion (but it does not have to be...)

Built into the profession of trading is the potential for loss and pain so great that you can come to the conclusion that you cannot go on. However, there are steps that you can take to prevent this from happening. If you are in the midst of the full-blown catastrophe and you feel yourself snowballing, that is the time to immediately lighten up on your responsibilities and simplify your life. Go from the physical to the bigger and more substantial things in your life such as primary relationships, your family, and closest friends. If you have already lost the money in a trading suicide, or you are in the hospital because you have already attempted to end your life, you can use this moment to convince yourself that your life is over and futile. On the other hand, you can use this experience as a wake up call to convince yourself that you do not want to get to this point ever again.

SECTION 7
Choosing Success

Chapter 30

The Magic Formula

Close but no Cigar

The first step in creating great success is finding the formula that is exactly right for you and your unique situation. Before he found his perfect recipe for success, Hershey went bankrupt so many times that he could have written a manual on how to fail - except that he never stopped until he found the magic formula. Up to that point, despite all of his years of hard work and good intentions, he was not eligible for the kudus that would come from just a minor tweaking in his approach. Once he found that formula, though, the world recognized his "genius." Thomas Edison failed forty thousand times until he found the right filament for the light bulb that made him rich and famous. Up to that moment, he was engaged in a failed enterprise.

When a trader achieves great success, it is usually a result of having found his own magic formula. That formula may look familiar or it may be totally unique to the individual trader, but it is the one that works for him.

Don't Mess with Success

It is one thing to achieve great success, but can you maintain it? The first step in sustaining great success is to not mess up the formula. If it works, and it works brilliantly, leave it alone. Unfortunately, for people who have the motivation to be highly successful, it is probably harder to keep from abandoning the formula than it is to find it in the first place.

Boredom or the need for change and a new challenge can seduce a trader who loves to do research and create new systems. Sometimes, though, a trader is not even aware of his own magic formula or he may forget the magic ingredient or combination of ingredients to his success. When that happens, his trading falls apart and he is at a loss to understand what happened. And sometimes, events occur in a trader's life that change the conditions in his life so much that all the ingredients are still there but the formula cannot work.

On Top of the World

As one of the partners in a very successful trading firm, Ken earned an annual income in the seven-figures. Ninety-five percent of the time, he was working at peak performance. Not only was his professional life picture-perfect, his home life was extraordinary. It is true that his teenage son was a little weird with his green spiked Mohawk and his daughter was somewhere out there in space idolizing the Back Street Boys. In spite of their minor adolescent rebellions, Ken had a special relationship with both of his children. But the center of his life was Karen, Ken's wife of nineteen years. Karen was the most loving, supportive, beautiful and intelligent mate a man could imagine and the envy of every man who met her. While Ken was on his long and rocky road to success, Karen supported the family, gave birth to their children, and cared for their home. At my seminar, Ken extolled Karen's virtues. "I am the luckiest man in the world," he said.

That was then but just a few weeks later, Ken met a woman on a business trip who rocked his world. By the end of two months later, he had left his family and moved in with his new love. Five months after that, Ken's life took a nosedive. While his wife sued him for her share of their assets, his new mistress proved to be selfish, demanding and controlling. Her meddling in his personal and professional life created a rift with his partners. Her lack of personal discipline freed Ken from his own life-long pattern of personal disciplines and his trading fell apart. Now, Ken is on a course to financial disaster.

Ken's extraordinary success came after he had finally found his own magic formula that allowed success to flow. His road to ruin resulted from abandoning that formula. In the world of modern science, when a biochemist attempts to duplicate the results of an experiment he found in a scientific paper, he may fail and fail until he finds that magic protocol, that series of steps that he takes in exactly the right way and then, wallah!!! Success! If he attempts to change that protocol in any way, he will once again fail to get his experiment to succeed. The same thing can happen to a trader with a magic recipe for success.

New and Improved – The Benefits of Tweaking…

Does this mean that you can never make changes in that magic formula? Of course not. Conditions that made that formula work can change so that the formula no longer produces results. In that case, you must be willing to update the formula to meet current conditions. For example, market conditions that once made a trading system unbeatable can change so that your system no longer is profitable.

Tweaking means that you are looking for a way to improve an existing formula so that you can benefit from what has worked and find out what can be made more effective. It is the very opposite of throwing out the baby with the bathwater. Sometimes tweaking is necessary for an old formula to keep producing results. For example, your old trading system may simply lose momentum over time and tweaking it can bring new life to its performance. Tweaking can include adding a new ingredient to the mix or modifying behaviors.

If your trading needs tweaking, you can look back over what you have created and check for ways you can improve what you have done. For example, you can look at your back-testing to see what the results would have been if you had done something differently. Suppose that you changed the stop or the size of your trades, or the times you trade, or added an intuitive indicator over and above your technical indicator – what would be the results?

A Cash Cow Gets no Respect

It is true that formulas can be improved on, but the delicate balance of success and failure must be considered with each change. My father owned a diner many years ago in New York called the Boulevard Diner. It was a simple diner that served excellent food, and it was the original cash cow. But my father was never satisfied with what he had in that incredible success. He wanted a fancy restaurant. He didn't want a cash cow; he wanted a cash thoroughbred. So, he opened one fancy restaurant after another, all of which failed.

Many years ago, I knew a trader named Derek who had figured out a way to make a very substantial living. He had figured out how to find numerous small clients by giving free seminars through local community centers. Convinced that he was a business genius, Derek decided to branch out. After all, he reasoned, if he could make this much money by working through little community centers, imagine what he could do if he charged money from large clients.

Once again, the cash cow seemed too mundane, too predictable and limited. So, Derek turned his back on the community centers and developed a very sophisticated marketing scheme. The only problem was that it did not work. Despite years of working and reworking his new approaches to marketing, Derek never again reached his former level of success. To this day, he continues to try to find a winning formula. Recently, he mentioned that he had considered going back to his old strategy, only to find that the doors were no longer open to him. He had strayed from the magic protocol and there was no going back.

Family and the Magic Protocol

The old adage that "you shouldn't fix it if it ain't broke" came into being long ago and has stayed in our lexicon because it contains a great deal of truth. Ken, our multi-million dollar trading partner had a magic formula that was more like a herd of cash cows than my father's Boulevard diner. Despite his public protests of devotion, he had come to a point in his life where he was looking for something new and exciting in his love life. The problem for Ken was that it never occurred to him that his family was an essential ingredient in his magic formula for the great success he enjoyed. Somehow he had forgotten about the amazing self-sacrifices that his wife had made for him, and the tremendous support she provided him. Her hard work at home freed him up physically and emotionally to have the clear head he needed to trade at a peak performance state.

Over Extending

When a trader named Josh, who derived his sense of security and comfort from living on a fixed income, was pushed out of his comfort zone by a new mortgage and a growing family, he stopped trading as well as he did when he felt secure. To function at peak performance, like Josh, many traders need to feel secure and in control. The delicate balance in the magic formula is upset for these traders when they over-extend their finances. The irony for them is the fact that they are getting what they thought they wanted, but, in the process, they are sowing the seeds for losing what they have achieved.

What to do With all That Milk?

What does this mean for traders who have found the "magic formula" and begin to feel bored by it or confined by it. Should they never turn in that simple country cow for a much larger, finer, more sophisticated city bovine? Should they live in fear that any changes and/or improvements will ruin the formula? All good questions...

The first step is they must determine first what the magic formula actually is. Not everything a trader does and not every condition in his life contributes to that magic formula. There are usually a fair number of things a trader can change or improve upon without affecting the formula. In fact, there are usually a fair number of things that can be tweaked to dramatically improve the formula. The problem is that unless you understand what it is that has brought you your success, you are more likely to lose respect for its value to your happiness and success.

The second step is to figure out why you feel a need to make changes. What is lacking in your life? If you need more excitement, perhaps a change in your trading is not the arena for taking new risks but a new hobby may be. If you are feeling a lack of vitality and you think that you need a major change, perhaps an improvement in your diet would help, or a membership in a gym or joining a sports team for adults. If you are feeling that your trading is no longer on target, you may need to take some seminars, read some new books, or find a mentor or coach. If you are feeling dissatisfied with your marriage, rather than break up your marriage and leave devastation in your wake, you could seek marriage counseling or spend more time with your spouse and rediscover what made you fall in love in the first place.

The third step is to work out a plan of action. A plan needs a goal, so you need to verbalize the reason you want to make changes and what you are hoping to achieve. One of the best tools is to redesign your business plan and to continue to update it on a regular basis. This strategy allows you to see what it is that you have done, what has worked in the past and where you want to go in the future. As a result, you will not be flying without radar, simply reacting to a need for stimulation and change.

Conclusion

Successful traders are likely to discover, over time, an urge to change their magic formula without realizing that they are preparing to kill the goose that laid their golden eggs. Rather than take drastic steps that result in sad results, itchy traders can take a series of smaller steps that can bring about positive changes. But first, they need to know what it was that brought them success in the first place and preserve its essence for their future well being.

Chapter 31

KNOWING WHERE TO TAP

Over the years, traders have pointedly asked why should they spend so much money for Neuro-Linguistic (NLP) counseling to solve their trading problems? A fair number of these traders have gone through traditional therapy, taking months or years, of weekly and bi-weekly sessions that are relatively inexpensive per session. If these same traders have not achieved the results they wanted through such an extended therapy, how can I justify asking for a major financial commitment for two days of work? An excellent question, I will begin my answer by telling one of my favorite stories:

A ship breaks down just before getting ready to take off on a long trip. The engineers try all of their usual tricks to get it started, but nothing works. Just then, a clever but naive young engineer decides to look in the yellow pages. He remembers a TV commercial that said that you could find anything there. Low and behold, he finds an ad for a man who claims that he can fix any ship. The young engineer called this Mr. Fixit and told him that many people would be grateful if he would come to look at the ship and see what he could do. Soon, the man appeared on board. With only a hammer in hand, he descended to the boiler room, and appraised the situation for a long minute. Then, he lifted his hammer and tapped. Immediately, the ship started. While everyone was jumping with joy and gratitude, the man reached out his hand and said, "That will be a thousand dollars." In disbelief that anyone would charge a thousand dollars for one minute's work, the captain shouted, "I want an itemized statement!" "Absolutely," replied the man, scribbling out an invoice and handing it to the captain. The invoice read,

$ 1.00 for tapping
$999.00 for knowing where to tap

Psychological Changes Happen Instantly

Just as it is important to know where to tap to get machinery to work, it is important to know where to tap when you need to get people to work efficiently and effectively. All dramatic psychological changes take place in an instant. Getting to the point where that change can take place is what takes time. How much time it takes for the dramatic change to occur depends on the facilitator's experience, training, and knowledge to determine where and how to tap - and on the desire of the client to allow it to happen. This principle forms the basis of Neuro-Linguistic Programming.

Doing the "Trader Tap"

In spite of a good methodology, in the end, a trader's success is all about his ability to tap his psychology into taking the trade. When a trader has psychological blocks because of fear, he will sabotage his method and himself. The decision-making moment is defined by a trader's ability to face the demons of the past and the pictures he creates of failure or success in the future. Just like a good tap dancer flows from one step to the next, the same flow has to exist for a trader to get the most out of his system.

Michael was a good trader, but when he had a high level of stress, he would revert back to being a vulnerable child. This pattern created indecision and sabotaged his results. When Michael first started trading, these stressful moments would occur as infrequently as once a year. After years of trading, however, he began to suffer from episodes as often as twice a month. He called me when these episodes began occurring even more frequently. Michael had good reason to develop more stress in his life. His new baby son was diagnosed with autism and the child's condition absorbed all of his wife's attention, making her exhausted and depressed. When Michael came home at night, his wife made his life miserable through her complaints and demands.

In addition to dealing with Michael's present situation, we also had to deal with the issues from the past that caused his moments of sabotage.

One-Upmanship

When Michael spoke to me about his life, it would seem by his programming that he should have been destined for greatness. There did not seem to be anything that would hamper great success, but intuitively I felt that there was. So, I did what I call "one-upmanship counseling." This is accomplished by going through a series of stories about issues that other traders have had that have held them back and watch for some reaction. When a client feels compelled to speak about a situation that is similar in his life, I listen. Michael's unconscious responded. He talked about an incident from his childhood where a summer camp counselor took him aside and proceeded to coerce him into inappropriate behavior. As Michael spoke of this incident he was detached from his feelings, as if the incident had no effect on him. Later, in an altered state, this situation proved to be traumatic and the cause of his not feeling worthy of achieving success.

Learning Where to Tap

I started studying psychology while going through a difficult divorce. My husband was suffering from the psychological effects of serving in the Vietnam War. Feeling helpless and vulnerable, I decided that I needed to understand the workings of the mind. I wanted to understand how a normal human could instantly change into a troubled person by experiencing one or more horrifying moments. If a person could change in a negative way so quickly, I was convinced that he could change quickly in a positive way, as well.

At first, I investigated various forms of "talk psychology." In typical "talk psychology," a person needs to discover "why" problems occur. This discovery period can take a long time. Too often, the discovery has little effect on making dramatic changes. Then, I started studying hypnosis and found that while it was useful, it had to be used in conjunction with other types of psychology to be effective. Ericksonian hypnosis led me to Neuro-Linguistic Programming (NLP.) While I have found that all forms of psychology have been useful for me to study, NLP is the fastest and most effective way to make changes. Once a skilled NLP practitioner learns how people have programmed themselves, knowing where to tap makes dramatic change immediate and effective.

Vietnam Revisited

In working with traders, I have often revisited the horrors of Vietnam. Many of the men with whom I have worked have gone through years of therapy, only to have nightmares and daymares that continued to affect their lives. Recently, I received the following e-mail from a client who had come for work after experiencing years of war flashbacks and trading sabotage. Peter has allowed me to quote from his letter:

> "First of all, I must tell you that since I saw you, I have had NO, NONE, ZERO, ZILCH FLASHBACKS, and my decision-making ability has returned to peak form. Even my wife tells me the money was well spent. I just wish I'd done it sooner. Last year was my best overall business year since I started my own business. .."

As dramatic as the results are that this letter spells out, it is by no means extraordinary. Of course, Peter was highly motivated, and a client's motivation is the second most important ingredient in the formula. But, once a trader makes up his mind that he is willing to work on the issues that are blocking his success, there is no stopping him when he applies the right method.

So, here are the questions you might want to ask yourself:

1. Do I have a trading block or pattern of self-sabotage that is preventing me from reaching my goals? If you are unsure of the answer, you can answer in the affirmative if you have a pattern of giving back to the market as much or more every time you have a successful trade or series of trades; or if you have done everything you need to do and more to create a successful trading business but continue to fail to reach your objectives; or if you find yourself engaged in self-destructive behaviors such as gambling, excessive drinking, taking drugs, putting your marriage and home in jeopardy, abusing your health, etc.

2. Have I been putting off dealing with this problem because I believe that I cannot afford the time and money involved?

3. Do I lack confidence in anyone's ability to help me? Have I had a bad experience in the past (or someone close to me has had a bad experience) in which I spent a lot of time and money in counseling, without the benefit of a major change in the problem?

4. Could my trading results benefit greatly from a process that could transform a long-standing problem, issue, or pattern if that process were very fast and effective? In other words, how much money am I losing and how much money am I failing to make each year because of these unresolved issues?

5. Am I willing for a change to take place, and to do whatever I need to do in my own attitudes, beliefs and behaviors to ensure that it is a lasting change?

6. Or do I have too much at stake in maintaining the status quo, regardless of how much unhappiness it creates for me and those closest to me?

The Bottom Line

The bottom line in paying for a counseling service should be the same one a trader applies to any of the many services and support systems he buys. What is the risk-reward ratio? In other words, how does the cost of the service I'm paying for compare to the financial benefits it confers? If you are paying more for a service than you are benefiting financially from it, it is a bad investment. If, for example, you pay a thousand dollars for a trading service and you see no incremental increase in your profits, you have made an unwise investment. On the other hand, if you invest in a resource that increases your profits many times that investment, you have chosen wisely.

Last year, I had a highly motivated client who increased his trading results from $75,000 annually to $3,000,000 in the first year and over $10,000,000 annually in the second year. If you think that these results represent a major benefit from money expended, you are quite right. Do you think a weekend of hard work with an NLP counselor was a wise investment for him? Do you think that he made a solid commitment to getting results and maintaining them? While this particular client was unusually motivated, it is not unusual to see dramatic improvement in trading results after counseling.

Finding the Right Counselor

As much as I would like to say that I am the right person to help every trader, this is clearly not the case. In order to find the person who knows exactly where to tap, each trader has to find the right counselor who is the right fit for him and for his unique situation. Just as I do not accept everyone who calls as a client, a trader must have a solid set of criteria for selecting a counselor:

1. Does this counselor have a track record in working with traders who have similar problems?

2. Have I checked his/her references and spoken with others who have worked with him/her?

3. Did someone that I know and trust refer me?

4. Have I heard this counselor speak or have I read anything he/she has written so that I know something about him/her?

5. Do I feel that we are compatible and that I can work with this person? Do I have enough confidence in this person to accept what he/she says and to do what I am asked to do?

Conclusion

If you are wondering how to solve a trading sabotage problem and you are reluctant to spend the money on counseling, you need to consider the cost of not working on your problems. Should you decide to continue on your present path, you need to consider what the cost is to you versus the cost of one-time counseling. But, remember this caveat, knowing where to tap in a trader, regardless of how much it costs and how quickly it can be accomplished, is a team venture. Unlike a piece of machinery, tapping the right place in a trader works quickly and efficiently, only if the trader is willing to do his part.

Chapter 32

_____

CHOOSING OPTIMISM AND OPPORTUNITY

Are the markets putting you in a negative state of mind? If so, you're certainly not alone. You were just beginning to feel a sense of stability and comfort in a bull market using a methodology that was creating a profitable income when the markets decided to weed the traders who were playing the pyramid game from the real traders. What I find most amazing is the fact that many traders realized that the markets were overbought, but still failed to prepare for an oncoming bear market. The traders who did prepare for the current conditions in the markets are cheerily calling me with what I call the "Optimistic and Opportunity State of Mind." As one of my clients recently said, "I know a lot of people are losing money, but we are still doing great."

Refusing to Participate

Recently, I read a book where the author was describing an experience that taught him a powerful message. At a gathering of real estate brokers during a recession, the author overheard many brokers discussing not having enough to survive and not knowing whether they could stay in the business. One individual in the group appeared to be happy and full of positive energy. The author said to this smiling man, "You are obviously not a real estate broker." "Yes I am," was the man's enthusiastic reply and he went on to say that business was great. After some conversation about the hard times in the real estate market, the enthusiastic real estate broker declared,

"I refuse to participate in this recession!"

The fact remains that there are people still making money in the markets despite its present steep decline. If you are not one of them, you are probably sharing your own doom and gloom stories and getting a lot of agreement from others. Or you could be one of the few traders who is saying,

"I refuse to participate in this bear market!"

The Double "O" Dilemma

It is easy to wake up in a positive state of mind when everything is going your way. The economy is good, you are making money and the world is your oyster. You can certainly feel justified in feeling bad when your old success strategies stop working and you can find a lot of agreement from people in similar situations. However, when your attention is focused on negativity, poverty consciousness, and being right about a difficult market, how you will be able to recognize opportunity when it comes your way?

Preventing a Larger Problem

Ronnie called me about two years ago. He was living a good life while making huge amounts of money. At that time, a recent tragedy had him concerned that he might reach a point where he would not be able to continue to support his family, his employees, and all the service people supporting his life style. Ronnie knew that he was benefiting from the bull market because his trading method was dependent upon an invigorated up market. Ronnie's new fear of loss was affecting his normal positive state of mind and he was suddenly creating losses before the bull market had run its full course. Usually, fear is a trader's curse, but in Ronnie's case it created a temporary setback that prevented a much larger problem.

Born an optimist, Ronnie told me that he saw opportunity all around him. Or at least that is how he remembered it. Because of his natural optimism, he had no contingencies in place for difficult times because he thought that any necessary adjustments would come easily to him.

One day, Ronnie received a call from his best friend's wife. Hysterically, she related that her husband had been in a serious car accident and that if he survived, it was unlikely that he would walk again. Ronnie watched as his friend disintegrated from being a top producing sales person and a happy-go-lucky family man into an angry, dependant invalid. This incident caused a new reality to set in for Ronnie. He began to feel vulnerable and started questioning his own ability to maintain his top performance lifestyle. Instead of staying in his normal "Optimistic and Opportunity State of Mind," he suddenly slipped into a "What if Everything Goes Wrong State of Mind." That is when he first called me.

The root cause of a trader's problem is rarely the obvious one. While his friend's tragedy was the catalyst that brought out Ronnie's fear, the root cause was buried deeply in his childhood.

When Ronnie was a child, he dreamed of having a dog. Ronnie realized his dream when Spot entered his life. One day, he found Spot dead. Ronnie's dog had been poisoned and young Ronnie was devastated. Although it could not be proved, Ronnie's family was certain that a neighbor who did not like children or dogs had poisoned Spot. The pain from losing his beloved Spot was great, but Ronnie was not going to allow his neighbor the satisfaction of seeing his anger and pain. So, Ronnie decided to bury his feelings and act as if the loss did not affect him. Still, Ronnie wanted to get even with this man. His father said, "You get even with people like this man by becoming very successful." His dad continued to say, "People like our neighbor won't be able to touch you if you are talented and rich." Ronnie's pain was so great that he was willing to try anything to stop it. Since he did not know of any other ways to stop his pain, he took his dad's advice. It worked. By focusing on becoming a high achiever, he kept his focus off of his grief. Many years later, his friend's accident brought into sharp focus the fact that all the money in the world could not protect him from being the target of tragedy.

Root Causes Waiting to Pounce

What I have discovered in coaching traders for the past 12 years is that even the healthiest and most successful minds can have potential sabotaging issues from childhood buried deeply within them. These old, unresolved issues are waiting for the opportunity to resurface and will do so in what appears to be unrelated situations and in the form of new issues. They then become the focal point of what needs to be healed. However, unless the core issue is addressed and transformed, the sabotaging issue will continue to reappear in new forms.

Feeding the Fear

What does fear look like? I am certain that you have dramatic and convincing stories of fear. Some are justified and real, but the sabotaging fears that I am referring to are those fears that look like the "monsters" of your childhood. You were convinced then and you are convinced now that those shadows of truth are something to be worried about. "But," you say, "The fact is I am losing money hand over fist, and will not be able to continue this much longer before I start to lose all that I have accumulated." You are right. If you continue in your current thinking and behavior patterns, you will definitely lose everything. Of course, it is not guaranteed that the most positive state of mind will overcome all of your problems. But, it is more likely to help than a negative state of mind. When you take the time to analyze your fear, you will realize that by feeding that fear with detailed justifications, you add to the problem and keep yourself from being in the right state of mind to come up with a solution.

You Attract What You Think About

The mind is a magnet that will attract to you what you think about. Many books have been written on this very subject. A couple of classics that come to mind are *Think and Grow Rich*, by Napoleon Hill and *The Magic of Believing*, by Claude Bristol. When you think about your fear, it will grow and when you bury your fear, it will find its way back to the surface. The only way to eliminate fear is to face it, allow it to express itself with appropriate emotion, transform it into something positive, and then do the things that a successful person does: follow or create a new successful model. The model that had to be re-established in Ronnie was the model that he grew up with: the Opportunity and Optimistic State of Mind. But, first, we had to transform his fears.

215

Climbing the Ladder of Success

To climb the proverbial ladder of success, the transitions between steps to reach the top step require the taking of risks. These risks might be the risk of major discomfort, uncertainty, and/or possible failure. People fail to reach the top step because they would rather not have to endure the transitions between steps. The first time Ronnie reached the top step, he was wearing blinders to the obstacles that were scattered along the way. His focus was on the success at the top. But when he had to make the climb again, he did not know how to deal with the transitions because he felt and saw the obstacles. He was more than happy to have me hold the ladder and guide his course.

While I cannot personally hold the ladders for all of you, I can give you some basic advice to help you keep the ladder steady for yourself.

Using a Negative Strategy to Create an Opportunity and Optimistic State of Mind

Since you have become so good at a strategy for creating pessimism, let's use this same model in reverse to create an Opportunity and Optimistic State of Mind.

- **The Pessimistic Model**
  You make statements to yourself like this:
    "The markets are terrible. There are no opportunities to make money. I'm going to keep losing money and I will not be able to maintain my lifestyle."

  These statements create pictures that look like this:
    Lines and numbers that look threatening. You see your family losing their home, with the furniture being carried to a small apartment. You see your children crying because they have to leave their friends.

  You start feeling like this:
    A knot in the pit of your stomach, a tight chest, and shaking hands.

- **Opportunity and Optimistic Model**
  You make statements like this:
    "If I was capable of coming up with a strategy for making money before, I am capable of coming up with one that will make money in these markets. If others can do it, so can I. If our family goes through a temporary financial setback, our love and support for one another will hold together the things that we cherish most."

  These statements create pictures like this:
    You are redesigning your method for trading. You get up in the morning with a bounce because you have the same passion that you had when you first started the business. You have a family meeting and they give you the support that you need to take you through the transition period.

216

You start feeling this:
Excited, fulfilled, loved, optimistic and ready for opportunity.

Coaching all Around

Yes, you will have temporary setbacks. A setback could come in the form of bad market news or from family and friends or associates who are pulling you back in the direction of your old, negative strategy. When this happens, it is important for you to be your own coach. Remind yourself that 'negativity thinking' is debilitating and only adds to the problem. Surround yourself with positive people who will help you on your constructive and positive course of action. If you need additional help, hire a professional coach who understands trading.

Ronnie Duplicating Optimism and Opportunity

The other day Ronnie called to tell me about the amazing results that changing his thinking brought into his life. He made the change as a child and again as an adult. His new plan works in a Bear Market and he feels that he can handle any fluctuations that the market might bring. Ronnie has also become a coach to his best friend who was injured in the car accident. With Ronnie's help, his friend has regained his confidence and enthusiasm for life by realizing that even though he is in a wheel chair, he can still be an exceptional provider, good family man and great friend. He decided to become optimistic about walking again despite what the doctors say.

Conclusion

Being in an "Opportunity and Optimistic State of Mind" is a choice. In order to maintain a positive state when life seems at its most challenging, you must coach yourself on a daily and, sometimes, an hourly basis. Choose a mindset filled with good thoughts and actions. Find a mentor or coach who continues to challenge you to stay on that ladder, dealing with the issues and obstacles that appear along the way.

——————

Chapter 33

JOY AND MAINTAINING SUCCESS

One of the questions that I ask investors/traders who come to me for coaching is, "What brings you joy in your life?" The answer to this question should just pop out. After all, successful investors/traders are highly goal oriented, disciplined, and ambitious people. How can you have those qualities in abundance and not know what makes you happy? Yet, strangely enough, a fair number of people cannot answer this question.

"Okay, Adrienne," you say, "suppose I'm one of those people who doesn't know what brings them joy...What does that have to do with making money in the markets?"

The answer is that if you do not know what brings you joy, it is very likely that you are not going to be able to sustain a long and successful career. Why?

The Things that Bring You Joy:

1. **Can Sustain You When Things go Bad**
   When you are having a bad day, when you have experienced a serious trading loss, when you are feeling depressed because a close friend died, when your son wrecks your car, or when you begin to question what life is all about, you need to have things in your life that bring you joy. It is important to know immediately what they are so that you can call upon them to remind you that life is still good, even when some things about life are going badly.

2. **Can Give You a Reason to Succeed**
   I know a number of individuals who gave up successful careers in the markets because they had no reason to be successful. There was nothing in their lives that they wanted to support, to nurture, and to see to completion.

3. **Give You the Energy, Enthusiasm and Perseverance to Keep Going**

Joy is the juice in your veins, the lift in your step, and the air under your wings. It's what keeps you working on that system and finding the answer to that nagging problem.

4. **Combats Depression and Pessimism**
   Negative emotional states can cause a trader to miss trading signals and fail to take advantage of opportunities. Pessimism can actually result in depression, and can also deepen and extend a depression. Depression, on the other hand can put a rapid end to a trading career.

5. **Make You a Joy to be Around**
   A spouse who only sees you when you are feeling joyless can begin to feel that you are a liability in her life. He or she may need to fill life with the company of those who make life happy and pleasant. After all, don't you want to be around people who are happy and can make you smile and laugh? A good and supportive marriage is one of the most important assets a trader can possibly have.

6. **Help You to Think More Creatively and More Clearly**
   Imagination works much better when the mind is at peace than when it is filled with miserable and obsessive thoughts. Great ideas and insights are more likely to come in moments of joy than when the mind is in turmoil. Opportunities seem to abound when you are happy and positive. These same opportunities will be difficult to see when you are mired in pessimism. The most successful investors and traders are able to use intuition as a reliable indicator in making trading decisions. Intuition is available only when your mind is at peace.

7. **Allow You to Feel More Joy in the Things that Normally do not Bring You Joy**
   There is a 'spill over' effect. When you are able to feel joy in one area of life, it 'spills over' into other areas of your life. This effect works in the opposite way when you are feeling angry, pessimistic and upset.

Recently, I worked with a client who began our session with a long series of sad stories and laments. Clearly, Charles' life had not been going well for some time. His wife had left him, his children avoided him and he had given up his career as a successful money manager. Charles was living with close friends who tried to encourage him to get on with his life and recommended that he call me. When I talked to him, he sounded hopeless. At a point in the conversation, I asked him what brought him joy in his life. He hesitated for a moment and barked at me, "What relevance does joy have to this conversation?" Did I not understand that there was no joy left in his life?

I was undeterred. Joy was the central issue for Charles. If he had nothing that brought him joy, it was unlikely that we would find an anchor to keep him from drifting further from a successful life. Without something to bring him joy, I would have a hard time giving him a reason to succeed. Without a fount of joy, I could not squeeze any excitement, energy or enthusiasm from him for the rigors of putting his life back together.

When Charles and I got together for private work, I pressed him to go back to times in his life when he was doing things that made him happy. It turned out that he had loved to play the saxophone when he was in school. He had also loved to read historical accounts, especially ones about submariners in World War II. In his childhood, he had lived in Connecticut and had loved camping in the woods. As we progressed, he began to discover that there were many things that had once brought him joy that he had slowly abandoned or forgotten. I convinced Charles to spend time walking through the beautiful North Carolina forests near his home, dusting off his old saxophone and starting to play it again, and going to the library to find some of the newer history books and accounts from World War II.

Without conscious thought, Charles began to find a new energy and passion for getting back into the trading game. With his new sense of worthiness, associates who knew his ability as a money manager were eager to invest their capital with him when they saw that the old Charles was back. He is now earning money for his clients and has made positive steps to change his whole life. When I saw him several days ago, he had a bounce in his step, he was dressed like a winner, and he was filled with a sense of optimism. Charles is well on the way to recovering the success and happiness in his life. The lesson for him is that if he had allowed himself to do the things that had created joy in his life, he would not have reached the bottom.

Like Charles, if you cannot answer the question, "What brings you joy in your life?" Then, you can also look back to the days when you were carefree and spent time doing the things that made you happy. As you begin to list them, you will discover that the list will begin to expand rapidly. Check off three simple things that you would like to add back into your life, and then go for it. You will be amazed at the 'spill over' effect on your work in the markets.

Conclusion

If you can figure out what brings you joy, then you can focus your thoughts and energy on those things in your life. The resulting positive energy will seep into the rest of your life, including your investing and trading and will open up new opportunities for success.

**Adrienne would like to thank
the following magazines and newsletters
that have published articles and interviews:**

Financial Trader

Futures Magazine

Money World

Technical Analysis of Stocks and Commodities

The Bridge Trader

The Sentinel

The Individual Investor

The Technical Trader

Trading on Target Newsletter

Traders' Catalog and Resource Guide

OTHER SERVICES & PRODUCTS

From Adrienne Laris Toghraie

SERVICES

- **Private Consulting**

  Remove the Barriers to Each Level of Success in Trading and All Areas of Your Life

- **Institutional & Corporate**

  Increase Production, Trading Ability and Teamwork

SEMINARS

- **Trading on Target**

  For Discipline & Overcoming Sabotage

- **The Winner's Edge**

  Gain the Technical & Psychological Tools for Becoming a Successful Investor

- **Intuition/Discretionary**

  Develop & Use Reliable Intuitive Indicators

- **Building a Capital & Client Base**

  Build Sales, Increase Production

- **Creating Affluence**

  Increase Resources & Balance Your Life

- **Enriching Life Seminar**

  Build Success by Making Better Choices and Gain Control Over Your Life

PRODUCTS

Trading on Target Home Study Course

(can be purchased in packages, as individual products, or purchased as an entire course)

Traders' Secrets Package
- Traders' Secrets Book
- Evaluation & Consultation on Phone
- Stress Relief Cassette Album
- 1 year subscription to TOT Newsletter

The Winning Edge Package
- The Winning Edge I Book
- Discipline 1 Cassette Album
- Six Steps to Greater Success Video

The Discipline Package
- The Winning Edge 2 Book
- Discipline 2 Cassette Album
- Get A Life Book

Business Plan Package
- The Winning Edge 3 Book
- Business Plan
- Discipline 3 Cassette Album
- 1 year subscription to TOT Newsletter

Interview Package
- Trading on Target 3 Interview Cassette Album
- Trading on Target 4 Interview Cassette Album
- Dear Coach Book

For additional information please contact us. Be sure to ask about the savings available when you purchase one of our packages.

Trading on Target
100 Lavewood Lane, Cary, NC 27511
Call (919) 851-8288 Fax (919) 851-9979
Website: tradingOnTarget.com   E-Mail Adtoghraie@aol.com

Visit our Website at <u>http://www.tradingontarget.com</u>

**Trader's Coach - Every Week New Solutions
to Discipline Problems**

Questions from Traders Answered

Special Packages

Upcoming Events

Make an Active Choice to Become a Top Trader

Visit our Website at http://www.traderspress.com

•View our latest releases•
•Browse our updated catalog•
•Access our Gift Shop for investors•
•Read our book reviews•

Contact us for our hardcopy 100 page çatalog.

TRADERS PRESS, INC.®

PO Box 6206
Greenville, SC 29606

Tradersprs@aol.com

800-927-8222

864-298-0222

Fax 864-298-0221